Lyonesse

Penelope Skinner's plays include *Friendly Monsters* (MTC online lockdown reading), *Angry Alan* (Underbelly/Soho), *Meek* (Traverse/Birmingham Rep), *Linda* (Royal Court/MTC), *The Ruins of Civilisation* (MTC), *Fred's Diner* (Chichester Festival Theatre/Magic Theatre, San Francisco), *The Sound of Heavy Rain* (Paines Plough/Crucible), *The Village Bike* (Royal Court/MCC), *Eigengrau* (Bush) and *Fucked* (Old Red Lion/Assembly Rooms). For *The Village Bike* she was the recipient of the 2011 George Devine Award and the 2011 Evening Standard Charles Wintour Award for Most Promising Playwright. For *Linda* she was shortlisted for the Susan Smith Blackburn Prize and was the winner of the Berwin Lee Award. For *Angry Alan* she was the recipient of the Edinburgh Fringe First Award.

PENELOPE SKINNER

Lyonesse

faber

First published in 2023
by Faber and Faber Limited
The Bindery, 51 Hatton Garden
London, EC1N 8HN

Typeset by Brighton Gray
Printed and bound in the UK by CPI Group (Ltd), Croydon CR0 4YY

A CIP record for this book
is available from the British Library

978-0-571-38912-4

MIX
Paper | Supporting
responsible forestry
FSC
www.fsc.org   FSC® C013604

Printed and bound in the UK on FSC® certified paper in line with our continuing
commitment to ethical business practices, sustainability and the environment.
For further information see faber.co.uk/environmental-policy

4 6 8 10 9 7 5 3

Lyonesse was produced by Sonia Friedman Productions and first performed at the Harold Pinter Theatre, London, on 17 October 2023. The cast was as follows:

Elaine Kristin Scott Thomas
Kate Lily James
Greg James Corrigan
Sue Doon Mackichan
Chris Sara Powell

Director Ian Rickson
Designer Georgia Lowe
Lighting Designer Jessica Hung Han Yun
Composer Stephen Warbeck
Sound Designer Tingying Dong
Casting Director Amy Ball CDG

Acknowledgements

Everything has changed since I first started writing this play. I need to thank the house in Cornwall, the people of Boscastle, and the lady in the tourist information office who sold me the DVD. Also those who came to visit me that summer: Bobby, Ginny and Alison. This play would never have existed in the way it does without Loretta Greco and the Magic Theatre in San Francisco, thank you for bringing such wonder into my life. Thanks to Nicholas Hytner and Will Mortimer at the Bridge Theatre. To Iman Qureshi for reading and encouraging during lockdown. To Bryony Kimmings and everyone from the workshop. To my agent Cathy King and all the team at 42. To the two Ws for inspiring me and making me laugh every day. To Laura Lomas, for creative solidarity, for being there at the beginning, and for the Halloween deadline. To Donald, for manifesting. To everyone who gathered on the Winter Solstice: Susannah Fielding, Anna Calder-Marshall, Jackie Clune and Bryan Dick. To Ros Brooke-Taylor, Jack Bradley, Matt Trueman, Emi Staniaszek and everyone at SFP. To Dinah Wood and everyone at Faber. Thank you so much to the absolute dream cast: Kristin, Lily, Doon, Sara and James. To Georgia for the beautiful design and the brilliant creative team. The most special thanks and gratitude to Sonia Friedman for championing this play and believing in it. And thank you to the wizard Ian Rickson for making all of this happen, and for being a kindred spirit.

For W. Magic

Characters

Kate
a development executive

Elaine
a retired actress

Chris
Elaine's neighbour, a poet

Sue
the studio boss

Greg Trellis
a film director

LYONESSE

Notes

/ indicates an interruption. The character on the next line
should start talking. The character whose line is interrupted
should keep speaking aloud.

The layout of shorter lines indicates patterns and rhythms of
thought and speech. You should be able to 'hear' them but
not as beats or pauses.

'Beat' indicates a short beat, a moment, not a pause.
Only 'pause' means pause.

(words in brackets) should be 'whispered'.

*

Stage directions which indicate physical action or, for
example, where a character is looking, should be considered
part of the text and adhered to.

Physical contact between characters not indicated in the text
should not be added casually.

Act One

Lilith Entertainment.

Kate, a woman in her thirties, has just entered, flapping around with a heavy overcoat, hair dripping, open handbag scattering items as she apologises. Sue, in her fifties, immaculately dressed and poised, stands by the window.

Kate Sorry sorry sorry sorry I'm so sorry! Greg's flight was delayed and the nanny's away and Izzy's been sick all weekend. I've had about ten minutes of sleep

Sue It's fine.

Kate had to wait for my mum to drive up from Surrey to take over, she got stuck in traffic

Sue Kate?

Kate and by the time I left it was pouring with rain and the tube was delayed and
god isn't it hideous out there? This time of year is just

Sue Shall we make a start?

Kate Right! Sorry I'm just
head's all over the place

Sue Please stop apologising.

Kate Sorry.
Sorry.
Let's make a start. Your hair looks amazing by the way.

Sue Thank you.

Kate I love that jacket.

Sue So.

Kate Right.

3

Sue Elaine Dailey.

Kate Yes. Yes! Exciting!

Sue You looked her up?

Kate I did. Yes! I can't believe I've never heard of her!

Sue What did you find out?

Kate I watched her entire sitcom on YouTube.

Sue About the woman herself.

Kate Yes! Sorry. Okay. So. Actually let me just get my notes.

Sue Sure.

Kate rummages in her bag. It goes on for quite a long time. Sue watches.

Kate I uh
oh you know what
I think I left them at home. Do you want to uh

Beat.

no it's okay. I can remember most of the uh 'Come on, Kate. Get a grip!' Hahahaha.

Beat.

Okay okay okay. So! Elaine Dailey uh
well obviously you know she's missing, right?

Sue You tell me.

Kate She's been missing for like thirty years. I mean
I'm assuming
but well okay so to begin at the beginning:
Elaine Dailey grew up in the North of England and caught the acting bug as a child. When she was a teenager she was appearing in local panto when she was spotted by a talent scout and invited down south to join the RSC. At the age of nineteen she was cast as Cordelia opposite the well-known actor uh Hal

uh
Hargreaves
and they got together. Hal was in his sixties at the time.
And married. Big scandal.

Sue Understatement.

Kate Hal left his wife. Elaine left the RSC under a bit of a
cloud and spent many years acting in the uh sitcom
I mentioned which at the time was a step down. Until she
met the director Clive Arbor, who is one of Greg's absolute
heroes by the way

Sue A legend.

Kate Arbor cast her in his seminal film *Crazy Dogs*. They
had an affair. Elaine left Hal. Not long after, Hal died, some
say of a broken heart. Although by then he was approaching
eighty, so
    either way the press were not kind to Elaine. She had a
small role in *Donna Volcano* another of Clive's movies but
struggled to get cast by anyone other than him until finally
she landed a big part in a West End show, uh, can't
remember which one

Sue Doesn't matter.

Kate she got rave reviews on opening night
    but the next day she suddenly just
    disappeared. The understudy went on in her place
    oh she's someone really famous now, what's her name?
    Anyway. I found a couple of old newspaper articles
basically suggesting Elaine had an attack of stage fright.
Some kind of hysteric fugue? There's also a bit of stuff on
the internet speculating she got murdered? But there doesn't
seem to be any evidence of that. There was no police
investigation. She just
    vanished off the face of the earth. Which I guess in those
days was easier?

    Beat.

Sue And?

Kate And that's as much as I

Sue But what do you think happened to her?

Kate I uh. Dunno. I guess stage fright is the obvious explanation but then
why has she never been seen again?

Beat.

Did someone find a body or . . .?

Sue You think she was murdered?

Kate Was she?

Sue laughs.

No?

Sue No but I'm delighted you think so.

Kate Do we know what happened to her?

Sue She's alive and well and living in Cornwall. This came via David Pritchett.

Kate The agent?

Sue Apparently he's known where she was this entire time.

Kate Huh.

Sue She's his client. Back in the day, she ran off to Cornwall and she's been lying low there ever since. Until now. She wants to tell her story and naturally she wants *us*
to turn it into a movie.

Kate She wants us specifically?

Sue David's recommended she come to us. I said to David obviously we need to hear the details first. See if it's something we can work with.

Kate Did he give you any sense of what the story might be?

Sue He was sort of making 'Me Too' noises.

Kate Oh really? Me Too who?

Sue All he said was: 'This is a story that must be told by women.'

Kate Please not Clive Arbor.

Sue God no. By all accounts Clive was an absolute sweetheart, may he rest in peace.

Kate Because just to say Greg would be devastated.

Sue I've got legals digging around just in case but my money's on Hargreaves. She was a teenager. He was sixty?

Kate Ugh.

Sue Or an actor in the show perhaps? Elaine won't breathe a word over the phone or in writing. She's apparently deeply paranoid. But if it is Clive Arbor then obviously this could be huge.

Kate They're both dead, right?

Sue I mean it would be *fine* if it was Hal but

Kate It can't be Clive Arbor though. Can it? Have you ever heard any

Sue Never! I've got legals digging around just in case but

Kate Greg would be devastated.

Sue It's got to be Hal. Surely. He was sixty, she was in her teens.

Kate Hopefully.

Sue Whatever it is. Something made her leave her entire life and vanish for thirty years.

Kate Poor Elaine Dailey.

Sue However, she is by all accounts not the easiest woman.

Kate Right.

Sue 'Eccentric' is the word David used. He also described her as 'struggling to maintain connection to the real world'. Apparently she swims in the sea. Every day. No matter the weather.

Kate Yikes.

Sue So. We need our cautious hats on. Take nothing at face value. But at the same time, we need to earn her trust. Softly softly et cetera. Which is why I think you're the perfect woman for the job. What do you think?

Kate The job?

Sue How are you fixed this week?

Kate In terms of –?

Sue What's your availability to meet with Elaine? She lives in a big house in the middle of nowhere. Got some funny name, I can't remember off the top of my head but Lucy can email you the details. You drive, right?

Kate I uh

Sue When's your nanny back? Or can your mum stay on for a bit?

Kate No well I mean Greg'll be home this afternoon. But

Sue Perfect. So you can get away?

Kate When are we talking?

Sue Tomorrow?

Kate *Tomorrow?*

Sue David suggested we all go down but I've got FIFHOP so I need a trusted envoy. What I'm thinking is, if this is something we want
    if she's a compelling enough character with a good enough story

and if you bring it in under a good enough deal
we could talk about promoting you. To exec.

Kate To exec the movie?

Sue If that's something you'd be interested in?

Kate I mean. I would absolutely love that. That would be

Sue Yes?

Kate Could we possibly make it next week? it's just really tricky for me to just
    up and leave Izzy at a moment's notice. / But I think if we could just

Sue Unfortunately, it's time sensitive. David's got a few offers circling. He's given us first look but he's keen to make a deal. He's worried she'll get cold feet, so

Kate Can I think about it?

Sue What's to think about?

Kate How to organise it?

Beat.

Sue I can ask Janine.

Kate No I just

Sue She's always hungry to get stuck in. Maybe this one doesn't float your boat.

Kate It does float my boat. I'm very – uh – hungry it's just usually the nanny uses the car so I don't have easy access to a vehicle so I'm like, 'Could I drive a rental?' or or and obviously Izzy's not been well so it's a question of can I leave her right now or –

Sue Can't Greg look after her?

Kate On his own?

Sue No?

Kate Can I just make a few calls?

Sue I don't want you to stress about it.

Kate I'm not stressing. / I want to do it.

Sue But if the timing's not right –

Kate No it is I mean it could be, I'm sure I can make it work, I just don't want to tell you I can go and then not be able to go.

Sue So don't go.

Kate But I want to go.

Sue I just need a decision either way.

Kate Okay I'll go. I can find a way.

Sue Are you sure?

Kate A hundred per cent!

Sue This would be a big step up for you, Kate.

Kate I know.

Sue I think you're ready.

Kate I think so too.

Sue Can I offer you some advice?

Kate Please.

Sue Sometimes there's this air of
   chaos

Kate Sorry

Sue don't apologise

Kate I'm really / sorry

Sue you don't need to be sorry. It's just
   we're all juggling the same challenges, Kate. The nanny.
The kids. The important husband flying off to god knows

where at the drop of a hat. There isn't a successful working mother in the country who isn't facing these struggles. Yes? Some of us are also trying to run a company and take care of our employees and after the past few years
    things are tough out there. Right?

Kate Right.

Sue I get it. We all get it. The question is, what do you want?

Kate I want

Sue Do you want to achieve success in your chosen field? Or are you just treading water till Greg makes enough money so you can sit back
    join the PTA
    have another baby
    head off on maternity leave and not come back?

Kate I don't
    are you asking me?

Sue Because here at Lilith Entertainment: we dream big.

Kate Which is why I love working here.

Sue No judgement. On any woman who wants to make different choices. Two husbands. Five dogs. Ten kids. I'll support your maternity leave as is my legal duty. Every time you want to have a baby. I'll buy you flowers and hire a temp and welcome you back with open arms. But when you're back. You're back. Yes?

Kate I'm back. I / promise.

Sue When we're in this office
    we are in this office. We are focused. We are prepared. We are professional.

Kate I'm so sorry I was / late, honestly Sue it just

Sue We don't apologise. We don't bring that
    in here. We leave that

out there. The guilt. The sick. The lack of sleep. That's for them. And in here, this space, this is for us. For our work. Together. As women. Creating, developing and producing female-driven stories which will change the world. Isn't that what you want to do?

Kate I do.

Sue 'Lilith are the visionaries.' That's what you said to me in your interview all those years ago. Isn't it?

Kate I did. And I meant it. We are!

Sue You reminded me of me. I thought: she's got what it takes to go all the way!

Kate Did you?

Sue I believe in you, Kate. I have always believed in you.

Kate Thank you.

Beat.

Oh god –

Kate is suddenly crying. Sue smiles.

I'm so sorry
    I don't know what's wrong with me
    it just means so much to hear you say that Sue because
    I'm such an admirer of you and everything you do and
    I'm very tired / and I just

Sue It's not a problem. Take a moment.

Beat.

I have another meeting so

Kate sorry

Sue Are we all set?

Kate Yes! I won't let you down!

Sue Thank you Kate.

Kate No thank you! Thank you so much for the opportunity. This is really, it's very exciting and I can't wait to get started!

By the time Kate has finished talking, Sue has already left the room.

2

Home.
Greg, mid-forties, statement glasses, indoor beanie, is holding a basket of laundry. Kate is looking at her phone.

Greg Cornwall? For how long?

Kate Couple of days. At most.

Greg A couple of days?! What's wrong with Zoom?

Kate I need to see her face to face. Build trust.

Greg So you can cancel Clive Arbor? Poor bloke's only been dead five minutes!

Kate We think it's more likely Hal Hargreaves.

Greg Clive Arbor is a legend.

Kate It's not Clive!

Greg Kate! I can't give up *Three Nights in Bermuda*! That film's one of my most definitive influences!

Kate Please can you not be negative about my project before it's even started?

Greg I'm not being negative. I'm just a bit
    I thought we had plans this week!

Kate Plans? We never / have plans.

Greg Not plans. Just
 you know.

Kate Oh.

Greg 'Agent Trellis. Ovum, incoming. Are you receiving, over?'

Kate Ha.

Greg How's your mucus?

Kate This is a big deal for me, Greg.

Greg Course it is but

Kate This is the promotion I've been banging on about since before Izzy was born!

Greg Kate.

Kate What?!

Greg Don't take this the wrong way but why are you trying to get a promotion right now?

Kate Because I deserve one? Because I've been at that company for years and I keep getting overlooked?

Greg Yeah but the timing.

Kate What about the timing?

Greg Sue's going to be pissed off if you take on a project like this and then go off on maternity. It's not fair on the company.

Kate I'm not pregnant!

Greg I know but you will be. Soon as we can spend more than five minutes in the same place at the same time without a two-year-old in the room!

Kate What was I meant to say, Greg? 'Sorry Sue I can't go because Greg wants to have sex'?

Greg Uh. 'Greg wants to have sex during the green zone on the egg tracker.' Yes I think Sue would understand that. Why not?

Kate It's not funny, okay? It's not a joke. It's my job.

Greg I've done all the laundry.

Beat.

Kate Thank you.

Greg And I was going to cook but

Kate No thank you.

Greg I brought you a nice bottle of wine?

Kate I'm on my diet, remember?

Greg Where are you going?

Kate I'm going to check on Iz then I've got to book a / hire car and

Greg Kate?

Kate I want to close my eyes before ten o'clock or I'm going to stress out about the drive.

Greg She's fast asleep.

Kate Is she?

Greg She fell asleep in my arms. So you don't need to 'check' on her. Just relax. Talk to your husband who you haven't seen for weeks and who has missed you very much. Hm?

Beat.

You should have seen her when I got back. She was so cute.

Kate Yeah?

Greg Gave me this massive cuddle and she was like 'I missed you so much, Daddy.'

Kate Did she? Aw.

Greg Her word formation is out of this world!

Kate Do you think so?

Greg For her age? It's spectacular. And she's so big! Time's going so fast!

Beat.

Since you won't be here tomorrow night. How about . . . we crack open that bottle of red. Head upstairs *before* dinner? Work off at least a thousand calories . . .
then get Deliveroo?

Kate How long ago did she go down?

Greg Or we could do it in here?

Kate On the new sofa?

Greg No?

Kate Also we'd have to spend more than two hours having sex to even come close to burning a thousand calories so

Greg Not the way I do it.

He grins at her.

What?

Kate I'm just not really in the mood.

Beat.

Is that okay?

Greg Of course! I'm not trying to
it's just last time
you had me on a sex schedule and a wank ban. This time I'm the only one even checking the app and now you're going for a promotion at work!

16

Kate Last time I wasn't even sure I could get pregnant. This time

Greg This time

Kate This time I know what happened last time.

Greg Babe. Remember what my mum said? The second one's always easier. When Rosie had Alfie she was only in labour for two hours and he shot out like a cannonball. And he was enormous!

Kate Please don't make light of it –

Greg I'm not, I promise! I just don't want the age gap to be too big! I want them to be like me and Rosie! Isn't that what we've always talked about?

Kate Yes!

Greg Otherwise they might end up like you and your brother. Never even speaking.

Kate Not because of the age gap. Because he's a bully.

Greg Maybe he's a bully because of the age gap! And anyway I thought we wanted a summer baby!

Kate We do!

Greg Then why / don't you want to

Kate I do want to, it's not that I don't *want* to but something's come up
at WORK. My work! You've been away for four weeks! Yes I want another baby but why don't you cancel a work trip for once, if you're so desperate to get me pregnant?!

Greg I can't just cancel a
let's not go there, please? / We always end up in a

Kate But you want me to cancel a work trip?

Greg Did I say that?

17

Kate You're trying to make me feel guilty!

Greg I'm not! I'm very supportive of your work trip!

Kate Doesn't seem like it!

Greg Well you're wrong because I am. I'm more than happy to look after Izzy while you go away for a couple of days. So long as Danneka's back, is she?

Kate She'll be back in the morning.

Greg So then it's no problem.

Kate Please don't ask her to do washing-up.

Greg She can do a bit of / washing-up while you're away.

Kate It's not in her job description.

Greg Why are you picking on me?

Kate I'm not picking on you!

Greg You're always like this when I get back. / It's so

Kate SHUSH! Was that her?

Greg I didn't hear anything.

Kate Have you got the monitor on?

Greg I can't find the plug.

Kate I thought I heard her.

They listen. There is no sound.

Greg You're hearing things. She's fast asleep. Look. Look at me. I know it's hard when I go away. And I know you always hate me a little bit when I get home. So, because I'm a very understanding husband, I will relieve you of your marital obligations on this occasion.

Kate Dick.

Greg So long as we get right back on that horse as soon as you're home. Okay? I'm just impatient to create our dream family! It's one of the things you love about me, isn't it? I get shit done! Now! I'm going to get you a glass of wine, then I'll leave you to work and tomorrow you will go away feeling completely fresh and prepared and

From upstairs, the undeniable sound of a child screaming. Kate slumps.

Kate I told you!

Greg I'll go.

Kate You said she was down!

Greg She was down!

Kate Clearly not!

He strides out. Kate disappears momentarily into the child's screams. Then:

Alexa: play power ballads.
Alexa?
Alexa! Play power ballads!

Alexa finds a playlist. Starts playing: 'When a Man Loves a Woman' by Michael Bolton. Kate stands, listening to the song.
Moments later, Greg comes back.

Greg She wants you.

Kate Of course she fucking does.

She storms out of the room. He calls after her:

Greg Love you! You're amazing! I'm so lucky to have you!

Greg stands, at a bit of a loss. The song plays on for a bit. Then:

Alexa: shut the fuck up!

Alexa stops.

Lyonesse.

Crumbling mansion by the sea. Old furniture, etc. A standing lamp and a shopping bag on wheels. Somewhere in the room, a large birdcage with an assortment of taxidermy birds inside. Canaries, budgerigars, lovebirds. The kind of birds you keep in an aviary.

Kate, looking bedraggled and stressed, is here, with a large leather weekender travel bag.

Elaine (early to mid sixties) is also here. She is wearing a swimming costume, giant welly boots, a swimming hat and a fur coat. She is holding an axe.

Elaine You're early.

Kate Am I? I thought I was late! What time did they say I was coming?

Elaine Tomorrow.

Kate Tomorrow? Gosh, I'm so sorry –

Elaine Where are the others?

Kate The others?

Elaine I was told to expect a whole party.

Kate Oh. No I don't think so. Just me. I'm the uh

Elaine I was planning a performance. To welcome your arrival.

Kate I didn't know.

Elaine There's a lot you don't know, Kate Trellis. Isn't that why you're here?

Kate Uh. Yes, I suppose so.

Elaine How was your journey? / Where did you come from?

Kate It was
a bit stressful. Long. I came from London.

Elaine London?

Kate North London.

Elaine London is very expensive.

Kate It is.

Elaine Is that where you live?

Kate Yes.

Elaine Who do you live with?

Kate I live with
my husband, Greg. And our daughter. And uh Danneka
who's like our uh well she's essentially our nanny. Au pair.
Type of thing. Are you chopping up a chair?

Elaine I am.

Beat.

You have a daughter?

Kate Izzy. Short for Isabella.

Elaine *Measure for Measure*?

Kate Sorry? Oh I see. No. I don't think so. Just my husband
loves the name, so

Elaine Huh.

Beat.

Kate Gosh look at these birds they're extraordinary. What
are they?

Elaine Those are my babies. My precious pets. Listen.
Aren't their little songs delightful? The way they flap their
wings up against the bars of the cage. I love them so. But

sometimes I feel guilty, wonder if I should just let them fly away, what do you think?

Kate looks at the stuffed birds, motionless and silent. Is Elaine winding her up?

Kate I don't know.

Elaine You alright?

Kate Yes, thank you. I uh – sorry, it's just the drive was uh

Elaine Oh yes. I don't drive around here. The roads are terrifying. I have to ask Chris. If I want to go by car. Into town or to the library. You can walk to the nearest shop though. For crisps or if you want a can of Coke. I used to work in that shop, but I'm retired now. You just go down the cliff path, past Chris's cottage, turn left, head down the little road, it leads you into the village. There's also a tea-shop and a hotel there. The hotel do a nice carrot cake and a good cappuccino. Do you like cappuccino?

Kate I'm more of a flat white girl myself but

Elaine You're a what?

Kate I uh, I looked at that hotel to stay in but David said

Elaine No! You must stay here! I insist!

Kate It's very kind of you.

Elaine I haven't made the room up yet. Do you want me to do it now?

Kate Oh no that's okay. I'd rather just get started if we can?

Elaine Get started?

The waves crash against the walls. Kate jumps.

Kate What was that?

Elaine Just the waves crashing against the walls of the house.

Kate Really? Is that
  okay?

Elaine There used to be a sea wall but it's eroded now.
I suppose one day in the future
  or indeed any day now should a big enough storm come in
  this house will just be washed away.

Kate Oh.

Elaine Not the sort of thing you have to worry about in
North London I daresay.

Kate No well. Actually there was some uh really bad flash
flooding near us last summer but
  we're up on the hill so it didn't affect us. We checked all
that before we bought the house. Flood risks and uh crime
rates and uh

Elaine What care you for a catastrophic event that doesn't
affect you? Hm?

Kate Sorry?

Elaine Why should I trust you, Kate Trellis?

Kate Why should you trust me?
  I mean
  I thought
  don't you want to adapt your life story into a film?

Elaine Actually I wanted to make it into a one-woman
theatrical extravaganza but my agent persuaded me it would
be more lucrative on the silver screen.

Kate Well. I'm really excited to uh
  I'm here because we'd love to hear the story. And then
I can report back to the production company about whether
or not we think we might be able to turn it into a movie.
It's not
  this isn't
  we should think of it as very informal. Just a chat.

Elaine Do you believe in ghosts?

Kate Um. I don't think so.

Elaine Oh dear.

Kate Why? Is it a ghost story?

Elaine No. How old are you?

Kate Me? I'm
   thirty-five.

Elaine Me too!

Kate Uh-huh?

Elaine Or thereabouts. Once I got to fifty, I started counting backwards. And of course, my playing age is mid-forties. On stage, I could even pass for a woman in her thirties. I swim every day. In the ocean. Did you know that? It drowns out the voices in my head. I do battle with the most powerful force on the planet
   and for that brief period every day
   the noise in my head goes silent
   and each time I swim back to shore
   it's a victory. I don't know how they're going to work around it once we start shooting but I suppose we'll have to put it in my contract will we?

Kate Your uh – ?

Elaine You know what directors are like. Time is money and all that!

Kate Uh

Elaine Today I was delayed because I took an extra sleeping pill last night so I stayed in bed for an awfully long time this morning then Chris came over to read me some poems then I thought I'd wait for the tide to come in and then you arrived
   unexpectedly early

Kate I'm sorry about that.

Elaine so I really must go before it's too late! Here

Elaine holds out the axe.

finish chopping up the chair and light a fire by the time I get back.

Kate Light a fire?

Elaine You do know how to light a fire?

Kate I don't, I'm afraid.

Elaine You don't know how to light a fire?

Kate I was never a girl guide or
is that
a problem or?

Elaine sighs a huge sigh as though, yes, in fact it is a huge problem.
She slams the axe into the chair. Kate jumps.

Elaine I did say to David that I would require a kindred spirit. And who do they send? A woman who doesn't believe in ghosts, who can't light a fire.

Kate Sorry.

Beat.

I do really want to hear the story. And I'm sure I'm going to be

Elaine Yes?

Kate I want to reassure you there has been a seismic shift in terms of attitudes to certain uh subjects and the focus is now very much on believing the uh
I don't want to say victim without knowing the details but let's just say progress has been made!

Elaine I see.

Kate You do?

Elaine What else? Tell me something else. About you.

Kate I uh
I like
pasta?

Elaine Pasta?

Kate I've gone blank.

Elaine No no no no. What's your story, Kate Trellis? What's your *story*?

Kate I don't have a story.

Elaine Everyone has a story.

Kate I don't have a
not an interesting story. Sorry.

Elaine Didn't say it had to be interesting. Just has to be honest.

Kate I am being honest, I don't know what to uh
I'm just a woman who works for a film production company.

Elaine That's a start. Good. How many films have you made?

Kate I uh
well I work for Lilith Entertainment, we're a company who produce films and develop visionary creators with a particular focus on centring women's narratives.

Elaine Didn't answer the question. How long have you worked there?

Kate Nearly ten years. It was one of my first jobs out of university, so

Elaine Which university?

Kate Oxford.

Elaine Oxford! Isn't that a story?

Kate I mean yes I went to Oxford but it was
  I suppose it was what was expected of me, if that makes sense?

Elaine Who expected it?

Kate My parents? My school? My friends?

Elaine Your friends?

Kate I guess I was clever? And I worked hard?

Elaine She's clever and she works hard. Oh dear.

  Beat.

You must like it at Lilith Entertainment, do you? If you've been there ever since your heady days at Oxford University.

Kate I did have a few other uh, before but I mean yes.
It's great. Great company. Brilliant people. They've been really supportive while I had Izzy which is unusual in this industry, so

Elaine Aren't you having any more? Everybody wants two point four, don't they? What do you want, a boy and a girl?

Kate My husband wants a boy. Yes. He's got an older sister so

Elaine A boy and a girl and a husband called Graham. How *marvellous*.

Kate Greg.

Elaine And what does Greg do? Hedge fund manager?

Kate He's a film director.

Elaine AHA! So that's why they sent you!

Kate Oh. / No I don't

Elaine Greg who?

Kate Um. Greg Trellis?

Elaine Greg Trellis? Never heard of him. What's he done?

Kate He's quite well known. Recently he's been doing this big TV action thing but his next project / is an independent

Elaine And how do you feel about being married to a quite well-known film director?

Kate I feel
  proud of him.

Elaine It gives you a certain status?

Kate Not because of that. Just because he's creatively interesting and and talented and obviously I'm happy he gets to follow his passion.

Elaine What about Izzy and the little boy? What's his name?

Kate No there's no
  there's only Izzy.

Elaine Is Izzy proud of Daddy?

Kate I uh um
  no Izzy doesn't care. I mean I'm sure she will one day. When she's old enough to watch his work, I think it'll be really exciting for her.

Elaine Have you seen my work, Kate Trellis? / My films? My situation comedy?

Kate Yes! I'm so sorry I should have said I'm a a a huge fan!

Elaine You probably watched them last night, did you? Your homework before coming?

Kate Not at all!

Elaine What about Hal Hargreaves. Have you heard of him?

Kate Uh-huh.

Elaine And Clive Arbor?

Kate Yes of course!

Elaine Of *course*!

Kate Greg's a big fan.

Elaine Of *course* he is. And you? Are you a fan?

Kate I'm
  not
  aware of a reason not to be? But I'm obviously keen to
hear what you're going to tell me about him. And about
Hal. About all of it really.

Elaine Is Greg your true love?

Kate Is he my true love? I would say so. In as far as I believe
in that.

Elaine You don't believe in true love?

Kate No I mean I'm sure I do I just
  sorry, I just wasn't expecting to have to answer this kind of

Elaine Oh you were expecting me to just pour my heart out
to you, were you?

Kate No no

Elaine So then, I'll ask again: is your husband
  the film director Greg Trellis
  the love of your life?

Kate He's the father of my child.

Elaine Not what I asked.

Kate This is a bit personal.

Elaine It's all personal, Kate. Did no one tell you?

Kate Sorry I just

Elaine You want to turn my lived experience into a movie,
but you thought I'd just, what? Shake your cold little hand
and spill my guts all over the kitchen floor for you to gobble
up and spit out if they're not to your taste? Well I'm so sorry
to disappoint you, Ms Trellis. And I'm sorry for your wasted
journey. I'm going for my swim. You can see yourself out.

Kate Wait, what?
      I didn't mean to
      Alright alright! Wait!

Beat.

Can we start again? I feel like

Elaine You can answer the question: or you can leave.

Beat.

Kate I thought he was the love of my life. When I married
him. When I had a baby with him. But lately I've been
      we're going through a rough patch.

Beat.

Elaine Go on.

Kate When Izzy was born
      it was a bit traumatic? And Greg was away? On a shoot.
So it's like he doesn't really
      he sort of doesn't believe it happened? And now we're
meant to be trying for another but I already feel like I'm
struggling? Rushing home for bedtime. Leaving for work as
late as I can. Rushing home again. If anything's even
remotely optional I give it a miss. Even the best
opportunities, I don't go. Whereas Greg. His career's better
than ever. He travels all over the world. Sometimes he
doesn't see Izzy for weeks on end but as long as he's
working he feels like a great dad! And Izzy adores him.
Never holds it against him. So you know, of course he wants
to have another because for him it'll be like
      double. Whereas I'm already half. So what's going to
happen if we
      am I just going to
      and I don't know if it's my hormones playing up or lack
of sleep or what but now every time Greg goes away, I find
myself having this fantasy that like

30

one of his car chases will go wrong or or or an explosion will malfunction
and he'll die?
And I'll get a massive life insurance pay out and never have to work or be married to
anyone ever again. Because if I'm going to feel this lonely all the time
then I may as well just be on my own!

Beat.

Oh god. I shouldn't have said all that.

Elaine Your neck's gone all red.

Kate I didn't mean it.

Elaine Didn't you? Gosh it sounded like you did. Do you think he loves you?

Kate Yes! Of course. I'm just not sure he really sees me.

Elaine Love doesn't make you feel unseen.

Kate I think love is more complicated than that.

Elaine You should sleep with Chris. Get your revenge.

Kate Who's Chris?

Elaine My neighbour!

Kate Oh the one who drives you places?

Elaine Correct.

Kate I don't think that's a good idea. Thanks though. For the

Elaine Chris is a poet. With the spirit of a dragon.

Kate He sounds great but

Elaine She.

Kate She?

Elaine She's one of the most extraordinarily beautiful human beings you'll ever meet.

Kate Uh-huh?

Elaine Her true love died.

Kate I see.

Elaine You can ask her about it tomorrow. She's an intrinsic part of my performance.

Kate Tomorrow? You mean?

Elaine I'm going to make your bed up. You wait here.

Kate Yes?

Elaine I'll come get you when your room's ready. Then I'll go for my swim. And tomorrow:
    I'll tell you my story!

Elaine leaves. Kate stands. Feeling as though a brisk wind has blown through her insides.

4

Lyonesse.
    Kate, holding a notebook, is here with Chris, fifties, a dishevelled air, wearing an old jumper and crumpled holey jeans. There is wine. As they chat, Chris prepares the room for Elaine's performance.

Chris Cheers.

Kate Cheers.

A long pause. Kate shifts awkwardly. Then:

So! This is exciting?!

Chris Yes?

Kate Haven't seen a show for ages.

Beat.

Elaine tells me you live down by the harbour?

Chris One of the little fisherman's cottages just before you get to the cliff path?

Kate Uh-huh? And uh
how long have / you been here?

Chris About ten years?

Kate Lovely.

Pause.

Do we have any idea what time we're getting started or – ?

Chris You got somewhere to be?

Kate No! Haha no no.

Pause.

Elaine said you're a poet?

Chris Elaine's been talking a lot about me.

Kate Oh no, we were just
she mentioned you give her a lift into town sometimes and uh

Pause.

I like the uh
birds. They're beautiful aren't they?

Chris I don't agree with keeping animals in captivity. I had a hamster once when I was a kid, it used to keep me awake at night
scrabbling around in the sawdust. Legging it round its plastic wheel. All it ever wanted was to escape. In the end I just took it in the garden and let it go.

Kate Wouldn't it get eaten by a cat or something?

Chris Wouldn't you rather be free and get eaten than live your whole life in a cage?

Kate I mean, I'm probably quite pathetic so

Chris Aren't you a film producer?

Kate I'm a development executive.

Chris That doesn't sound pathetic.

Kate Being a poet. Now that's impressive!

Chris Why?

Kate Why? Because well
not everyone can be a poet.

Chris All you've got to do is write a poem.

Kate Not everyone can write a poem.

Chris True. You could speak a poem. Or think a poem.

Kate I can't even think a poem.

Chris What if I'm a poet whose poems have never been published?
Is that still impressive?

Chris laughs loudly. Kate laughs a bit.

More wine?

Kate Yes please.

Beat.

So this house is amazing.

Chris You think so?

Kate Why's it called Lyonesse? (*She mispronounces it.*)

Chris Lyonesse. Name of a land which once stretched from here to the Isles of Scilly, but which sank beneath the sea. Swallowed by the waves in a single night.

Kate Huh.

Chris So the legend goes.

Kate You'd think a house like this would be damp but it's not is it? If anything it feels
   strangely warm.

Chris That's exactly what Elaine said. She said the first time she set foot in this house
   it felt like a refuge.

Kate Yes! Why is that?

Chris
   'When I set out for Lyonnesse,
      A hundred miles away,'

Kate Gosh really, where / were you

Chris
   'The rime was on the spray,
   And starlight lit my lonesomeness
   When I set out for Lyonnesse
      A hundred miles away.

   'What would bechance at Lyonnesse
      While I should sojourn there
      No prophet durst declare,
   Nor did the wisest wizard guess
   What would bechance at Lyonnesse
      While I should sojourn there.

   'When I came back from Lyonnesse
      With magic in my eyes,
      All marked with mute surmise
   My radiance rare and fathomless,
   When I came back from Lyonnesse
      With magic in my eyes!'

   Beat.

Kate Did you

Chris Thomas Hardy.

Kate Course it is! Sorry.

Suddenly, from the stairwell, they hear Elaine calling:

Elaine Chris?

Chris She's ready. Are you ready?

Elaine I'm ready! Are you ready?

Chris Hang on!

Elaine You're not ready?

Chris I got distracted!

Elaine By what?

Chris Kate Trellis!

Chris bustles round changing the lighting. She sets some kind of retro music player going. Pulls out a chair. Gestures to Kate –

Sit.

Kate Me?

Chris Who else?

Kate sits in the chair. She readies her notebook. Chris turns off one more lamp. Then:

Okay ready!

Elaine Ready?

Chris Lights! Camera! Action!

There is quite a long pause while the music plays. Kate, somewhat uncomfortable, realises that Chris is watching her. Then:
Elaine emerges from the stairwell. She is wearing a glittery mauve evening gown with huge feather shoulder-pads. Her hair (a wig) is a messy, piled-up mass of blonde curls. Maybe she's got a hand-held mic on a long wire.

Chris starts a round of applause. Kate joins in. Elaine smiles graciously.

Elaine Thank you, thank you. Thank you, all of you, for attending my little soirée. Let me first say a warm welcome to our new friends uh friend from Lilith Entertainment Production Company in London! Welcome!

Kate Thanks for having me.

Elaine Why do you have a notebook?

Kate Oh. I thought I might

Elaine Do we have a critic in the house?

Kate No god no, sorry, I was just going to
I'll put it away! Sorry. Sorry.

Kate puts her notebook away. Elaine nods. Then.

Elaine Presenting . . . The Story of Why I Went Missing. By Elaine Dailey.

Chris changes the lights. Elaine strikes a pose. Then:

Thirty years ago
give or take
I, the actress Elaine Dailey, meet the film director Clive Arbor.

Chris boos. Elaine hushes her.

I have been with my husband Hal since I was very young
too young, some said
so by the time I'm almost thirty, I have grown restless.
When I meet Clive

Beat.

sorry, when I
met when I meet Clive I am uh
I'm so sorry can I just

She takes out a piece of paper which has her lines written on it. Her hands are shaking.

37

When I meet Clive

I believe I have met the love of my life. I am swept away. He is the most extraordinary and brilliant man. It is the kind of passion I have read about in so many romantic novels. And Clive feels the same about me. He wants me by his side, all the time. He is possessive. Jealous even. Doesn't want me to take any work that doesn't involve him. I am his muse, he says. And he wants to keep me all to himself. Clive however

only works on screen, and my first love has always been the stage. In time, this becomes a source of tension between us. His obsession starts to feel like something else. Oppression. Suppression. And so one day

anxious to assert my independence, I audition for a leading role in the West End and am offered the part. Clive is furious. He tries various means to get me to change my mind before issuing an ultimatum: I must choose, he tells me, between him or the show.

Ha! At this, a fire bursts into life inside me. I tell him at once I am leaving. Pack my belongings, put my precious birds into a travel cage and move out. I stay with a friend for a couple of nights before renting a flat near the theatre. It is small. But convenient. Over the coming days, Clive sends friends to plead on his behalf. 'Clive is devastated,' they say. 'Won't you at least see him?' I try to explain the circumstances of our separation, but his version of events is already ringing loud in their ears. They all but accuse me of wanting to sleep with the director and/or several of my co-stars. It's complete nonsense. But with my history, who can blame them? I am shaken by the visits. Am I a dreadful, selfish woman? But then just as my resolve is faltering, rehearsals begin and

oh how it returns! Back here in the room I am strong, I am myself! And then

towards the end of the second week, Clive starts

following me. He waits outside the flat every morning. And after rehearsals at the end of the day. He tails me home. Lurks below my windows, long into the night. In the third

week, he takes to writing me letters. Love letters. Sad letters.
Angry letters. Threatening letters. And in the fourth week, the
phone calls begin. He stands in the phone box on the corner
of my street. All through the night. Begging and pleading and
weeping and screaming and warning that if he can't have me
   no one else will. He tells me if I stop picking up the phone
   he will kick down my door and murder me in my sleep.
'Does he mean it?' I ask my friends. They tell me 'of course
not. He just doesn't want to lose you. Poor man doesn't
know what he's doing.' In the final week, he disappears.
No more letters. No calls. I wish I could say it is an
improvement. Instead, I am on edge. Waiting to see what he
will do next. Because I know Clive. I know he hasn't given
up. Clive is relentless.

   Beat.

When you are afraid of the man you love
   something very strange happens to you. A kind of
   erosion. By previews, I am jittery. Jumping at shadows.
I lie awake at night, listening to every bump and creak,
imagining Clive outside in the darkness
   and only when it starts to get light, do I finally fall asleep.
It is exhausting. Overwhelming. I am determined not to let
this beat me but I fear I am failing
   falling. Crumbling. And then
   on the morning of opening
   I get word from the director. Great news, he tells me,
Clive is coming to the show! Tonight? Tonight! Such good
publicity. No? And quite suddenly and I'm not sure why,
I am consumed once again by the same spirit that made me
leave him in the first place. I cannot let him stop me. I will
go on. I must! And so I do. And I am, and I quote
   'magnificent'
   'spell-binding'
   'a force of nature!'
   I get so lost in the story I forget all about Clive and my
troubles and after the most spectacular show and filled with

that joyous adrenaline that comes only from making a deep connection with a live audience, I come back to my little flat thinking only of the future and

Elaine's throat tightens up. For a moment she cannot go on. Then, she takes a breath. And

and I find that the door has been kicked down and inside I discover
my birds
scattered around on the floor, their tiny feathery bodies quite cold and still. Their necks have been broken and I know
I know who did this
and I know why and perhaps
I can't be sure
perhaps he is still here
oh god. It is hard to describe my terror, as I gather up their lifeless forms and escape the flat. In fear for my life, I head to my mother's. What now? What am I to do? Should I telephone the director? The police? But as I imagine it, so the answer becomes clear: they will take his side. Every last one of them. I am alone. And this time his warning could not be more plain: 'Come back to me,' he means to tell me. 'Or you'll be next!'

Beat.

He knows where my mother lives, of course, and as long as she is protecting me, she too is in danger. And so the next morning, I sit with a cup of tea and the morning papers. I read every single one of my rave reviews
out loud
three times. 'Magnificent. Spell-binding. A force of nature.' I try to let it be enough. Try not to imagine the faces of my fellow company members this evening when I fail to show up for the performance. I cannot believe I am doing this, and yet
I take the road atlas down from the shelf
I close my eyes

I open a page at random to choose my destination. And I flee. I have no other ties. No

children. I tell no one where I am going except my dear agent David, and mother. I find this house and this house speaks to me. Tells me I will be safe here. And I start my life all over again. I save myself, but in order to save myself

I must lose myself. And surrender the thing I love doing most in the world: performing. It is, it was

She pauses, trying to keep control of her emotions.

a huge loss. Many times I have wondered if I made the right choice. I have missed so much. Friends. Opportunities. Mother's funeral . . .

Beat.

But David faithfully continued to represent me in secret

and we agreed that if something were ever to happen to Clive

well then my time might come again. But life being the way it is

only good things ever happened to Clive. And so, the years went by. Clive carried on making movies. I discovered sleeping pills. Clive won a BAFTA. I got a job in the village shop. Clive was nominated for an Oscar. I taught myself Moonlight Sonata on the piano. When he retired, Clive was given a lifetime achievement award for services to the British film industry. I got a state pension and a family size block of Fruit and Nut. But I learned to take pleasure in the small things. My daily swim. A cream cake in the afternoon. A poem read aloud by a friend.

Beat.

And then a few months ago, on a bright sunny morning

my darling David phoned to tell me that at last

Clive Montgomery Arbor had shuffled off this mortal coil. A heart attack. My first reaction was to weep. Perhaps a part of me still loved Clive. But in that same moment

41

another part of me came back to life! While the nation mourned, I rejoiced:

Clive was dead. Clive is dead. And I am alive. I am still alive!

And although I will admit it still makes me deeply afraid to say this

after all, I have been sequestered here for many years but I believe it is now time for me to speak my truth! It is time for me to step into the light!

Chris leaps up and changes the lights. Music starts.

Chris and Elaine sing a duet. Something faintly cheesy / unexpected, but which has great meaning to Elaine. Chris takes the opening verse. She sings like an enthusiastic child: eager to please, working hard to remember the words, forced gestures she has learned by rote. When Elaine sings, she is effortless, powerful, compelling.

When the music ends, a moment of silence. Kate, lost and not sure what to do, eventually starts clapping. They beam at her, eager for her feedback.

Elaine Thank you darling!

Chris What did you think?

Kate Amazing! Wow that was just

Chris We've been practising.

Kate I can see that!

Elaine What about the story? What did you think?

Kate Yes! Great! It's quite a story!

Elaine Is it worthy of a movie?

Kate I have so many questions but absolutely I think we can find a way to shape it into a

Elaine You think so?

Chris Is it what you were expecting?

Kate It is and it isn't.

Elaine In what sense?

Kate I don't know. I need time to process!

Elaine Process?

Kate I mean we need to work out don't we the uh the details but in essence I think this is a story we at Lilith Entertainment would be very interested in telling. The final decision will be down to my boss Sue but uh

Elaine But you think yes?

Kate I definitely think yes! Yes!

Elaine She said yes!

Chris I told you! I'll open the champagne!

Elaine I hope you don't think us presumptuous Kate, but we chilled a bottle just in case!

Chris This is it Elaine. You did it! You're going to be in a movie!

Elaine Elaine Dailey stars as herself in *The Elaine Dailey Story* coming soon to a cinema near you!

Kate You want to be in it?

Elaine Well of course I want to be *in it* darling! I'm making a bloody comeback!

> *Chris pops the bottle of champagne. Elaine whoops. She hits play on some upbeat, rhythmic music and starts dancing. Kate stays sitting. Chris hands Kate a glass of champagne.*

Chris Would you like to dance?

Kate Haha no thank you.

> *Chris and Elaine dance. Free. Kate watches. Imprisoned. After a while:*

43

Maybe I do want to. I said: maybe I do want to dance!

Chris What's stopping you?

Kate looks at Chris, and somehow, to her surprise, finds herself getting to her feet. She doesn't touch Chris, but does start dancing. Chris and Kate dance together. After a moment, the music changes. Something strange and slow. The sound of the sea crashing against the walls of the house.

Kate gets lost in the dance.

5

Cliffs / Home / Lilith Entertainment.
Next day. Kate, dishevelled, hungover, wearing Chris's boots, is out on the cliffs making a phone call. Greg appears, at home, in his pyjamas.

Kate Oh hey it's me. Were you asleep?

Greg No, no. How's it going?

Kate Yeah it's good. How's she?

Greg She's great! Danneka's just taken her out to the playground so

Kate Really?
Okay good. Sorry I missed your call last night I was uh working late and uh
what are you up to?

Greg I've got a couple of Zooms then I'm heading into town.

Kate Huh, okay. Okay. So it's all okay?

Greg We're fine.

Kate Has she been asking for me?

Greg Nope. She hasn't even noticed you're gone. And. Get this: she counted up to ten.

Kate She did?

Greg I think she's really exceptional, Kate.

Kate Well.

Greg Did you find out what the Me Too is?

Kate It's not really a Me Too but

Greg Who is it?
  Kate?
  It's not Clive is it?

Kate I'm afraid so.

Greg You're kidding.

Kate Yeah but it's complicated.

Greg What do you mean?

Kate I mean the thing he did. I'm not sure how to

Greg What did he do?

Kate I can't just

Greg Tell me!

Kate We can talk about it when I get home.

Greg Which is when?

Kate Well this is the thing. I might need to stick around a bit longer.

Greg Stick around? For how long?

Kate I texted my mum, she says she's happy to come and help out for a couple of days. Well / she's not *happy* but

Greg A couple more days?!

Kate Just till the end of the week.

Greg What about the egg?

  A beeping sound.

Kate The what?

Greg Our EGG!

Kate You're breaking up.

Greg We're missing the green zone!

Kate Hang on, Greg, / Sue's trying to call me!

Greg In two days we'll be back to / red!

Kate I've got to go, give Izzy a kiss from me
Hello?

Sue appears, in the office.

Sue Kate?

Kate Can you hear me okay? / It's a bit windy

Sue I can just about hear you. How's it going down there?

Kate Oh it's wild. I'm having a great time!

Sue What's that?

Kate How's FIFHOP?

Sue It's going extremely well, thank you. So listen. I got your emails.

Kate Oh yes?

Sue You were up late.

Kate Yeah sorry about that I uh

Sue Bit of a shocker eh?

Kate You mean –?

Sue My money was on pervy old Hal Hargreaves!

Kate Me too! I mean
not *me too* / obviously

Sue So listen! I had a little chat with Buddy Lindsey this morning at breakfast. Floated a few things off our slate and to my surprise this is what made him bite.

Kate As in, *the* Buddy Lindsey?

Sue Head of Pacific Studios.

Kate O wow.

Sue Turns out he's a huge Clive Arbor fan.

Kate Uh-oh.

Sue No no it's exciting! He's keen to hear more about the man behind the myth. And he said it doesn't have to be flattering so long as obviously so long as it's not libellous.

Kate Oh okay so

Sue Can you imagine?

Kate I mean

Sue Buddy money could get this over the line, Kate. Yes? But he moves fast and he doesn't like to be kept waiting so you've got to focus! We need something his people can read As Soon As, okay? Now quickly because I've got to head back in: I'm loving the stalking, that's all fab. But talk to me about the murder of the birds.

Kate Uh well, it's the well, the tipping point I suppose, the thing that makes her run. He killed her beloved pets.

Sue Uh-huh.

Kate It's a warning: you're next.

Sue Uh-huh.

Kate She was in fear of her life but she was scared no one would believe her so she just

Sue And we think he really did do that do we?

Kate I mean. She's got a big cage full of taxidermy birds in the house, so

Sue Sorry Kate, it's not a good line I thought you said a big cage full of taxidermy birds.

Kate I did, yes.

Sue The same birds?

Kate It's tragic.

Sue Is it?

Kate Sorry Sue I didn't catch that.

Sue What I'm asking is, is she a sympathetic heroine? Are we going to be on her side?

Kate I am. Aren't you?

Sue I'm still thinking about it.

Kate Did you find anything out from legals?

Sue Lots about Clive being demanding on set but nothing in terms of his personal life. None of his other wives have made a peep so what I've been thinking is
  is there a way to turn it into more of a
  you know like 'maybe it was all in her head' type of thing?

Kate In her head?

Sue Maybe he did it, maybe he didn't. Doesn't matter if he killed the birds or not, the important thing is she *thinks* he did. Hitchcock vibes. A psychological thriller.

Kate We don't want to say she's crazy.

Sue But is she crazy?

Kate She's eccentric. But in some ways . . .

Sue What?

Kate It's hard to explain. In some ways she's more sane than we are. The more you talk to her and spend time in her house, the more you start to feel like maybe you're the crazy one.

Sue Ooh. Love that. Goosebumps.

Kate Lyonesse.

Sue What was that?

Kate That's the name of the house.

Sue As in a female lion?

Kate No it's a magical kingdom. And a poem by Thomas Hardy. We should think about shooting here. And Elaine's going to be fantastic. She's so watchable!

Sue Fantastic in what sense?

Kate In the film. We're attaching her to star, right? She said

Sue She said what?

Kate She said David told us that up front, so

Sue I wouldn't worry about all that now –

Kate But did we tell her we were open to it?

Sue We are open to it.

Kate We are. / Oh great

Sue No promises but everything's on the table.

Kate I don't think she'll change her mind. And for what it's worth, Sue, she's very compelling. So beautiful and inspiring and I wish you'd heard her tell her story it was like
　　so sad but she's just so extraordinary at the same time you sort of want to *be* her!

　　Beat.

Are you still there?

Sue Are you feeling alright, Kate?

49

Kate Yeah?

Sue When are you heading back?

Kate I'm going to stay on till the end of the week.

Sue Really?

Kate There's so much in this.

Sue You can't follow up by email?

Kate This house is just the most extraordinary place, you know like I said
    we should shoot here. The views are breathtaking / it's got so much character

Sue You're cutting out, hun. Just send me a treatment, okay? Get the tent poles in place. Work out the shape.

Kate I've never been / anywhere like this –

Sue Oh you're back. Did you hear what I said about a treatment?

Kate Yes great!

Sue The man behind the myth!

Kate Can you hear me?

Sue No you've gone again. Kate?

Kate Hang on let me
    Sue? Are you still there?
    Sue?
    No you've gone.

Kate stands, taking in the view, breathing in the air. The cry of gulls, the wash of the sea.

6

Lyonesse.

Chris, wearing her coat, is scattering birdseed in the bottom of the cage. Kate enters, from the cliffs. In a room beyond, Elaine is practising the piano, scales and such.

Kate Oh hi.

Chris Good morning!

Kate I'm wearing your boots. I had to go up on the cliff to get signal and I

Chris Don't worry about it.

Kate What are you doing?

Chris Just feeding the birds.

Beat.

Kate Did you sleep down here?

Chris I guess I did. And now I'm leaving. Soon as I get my boots back.

Kate Sorry. God. I'm so sorry.

Chris chuckles. She watches Kate leap out of the boots, then flap around trying to line them up neatly. Then:

Chris How's your head?

Kate Not good. You?

Chris I've felt better.

Kate Um. Just checking but
Elaine did ask me to stay on for a few days didn't she?

Chris She did.

Kate I don't remember going to bed!

Chris No?

Kate The last thing I remember
ugh
was I playing the piano?

Chris Sort of.

Kate Because I can't play the piano.

Chris No.

They laugh.

Kate And why was there a swimming costume on the end of my bed?

Chris Elaine is lending it to you. For when you go in the sea? Like you promised?

Kate I promised to go in the sea? Are you sure?

Chris You do swim, I take it?

Kate Have you seen it out there?

Chris Wind'll die down in a couple of days.

Kate Maybe she won't remember.

Chris Maybe.

Kate There's no way I'm going in that sea. I'm not crazy!

Tiny beat.

Anyway! Good news! Greg's coping fine without me so I can stay for a bit and more importantly I spoke to Sue? My boss? She's at FIFHOP, this big film buyers' event? She's found a very important investor who's interested in Elaine's story!

Chris Huh.

Kate It's very exciting!

Chris And what about the directing. Did she go for it?

Kate Uh. Did she go for
oh god

52

Chris You doing the directing?

Kate Oh no. Listen that was

Chris So exciting!

Kate Ha that's very sweet of you but I shouldn't have we definitely shouldn't mention that to Sue!

Chris But I thought you said it's your dream!

Kate I said it was my dream for about five minutes when I was a kid but I promise you I'm not, I don't have the talent or

Chris You don't have the talent?

Kate plus I'm really indecisive. I just got swept away in our whole conversation about life and and and living our full potential but it's definitely not on the table for this project and we must never ever mention it to Sue. Okay? God! Why am I such an idiot?

Kate laughs, embarrassed. Then:

What other ridiculous things did I say last night?

Chris Well. You cried. And you said your life feels like a trap.

Kate Did I?

Chris You said you've spent your whole life trying to be someone you're not. Desperately seeking approval. Ticking off the boxes of achievement, hoping each time that something inside you will feel the acceptance and validation you long for. But you still haven't found it.

Beat.

And you told us you want to leave your husband because he's trying to force you to have another baby
   but you don't want one

Kate I remember now

Chris because last time

Kate I remember what I said.

Chris you nearly died.

Beat.

Kate He's not forcing me.

Chris To admit all that

Kate I wasn't 'admitting'

Chris it was very brave.

Kate It wasn't true. I was just
it's this house! This place! I don't know why it's just
making me . . .

Beat.

Chris When I first met Elaine
I'd just bought the cottage down in the harbour
I walked into the village shop
I only went in to get a pint of milk
she said 'You're new around here' and I suddenly found
myself telling her about my wife dying. And in turn, Elaine
told me about Clive. She said it was top secret. She said she
knew she could trust me. And she was right. I've never told a
soul. And she's never told anyone else since. Until now. You.

Kate Not because I'm me.

Chris She senses it inside you. You're an artist, Kate Trellis.

Kate Me?!

Chris Destiny brought you here.

Kate I work for a production company.

Chris Unleash your inner being.

Kate I'm not unleashing anything.

Chris You did last night.

Kate I was drunk!

Chris And now what? You think you can just go back? You can't! You're one of us!

Kate I'm really not! That wasn't some kind of truth I've been denying. I'm I'm I'm mortified! I should be being professional not not baring my soul!

Chris If it's not the truth, you didn't bare anything. You just made up a story about a woman who faced her own death
  nearly lost her child
  and since then has been forced to confront the uncomfortable realisation: that despite achieving everything she has always been told would make her happy
  she is now experiencing profound feelings of emptiness.

Kate stares at Chris. Then looks away. Chris watches her.

'Tell me about despair, yours. And I will tell you mine'

Kate I was drunk.

Chris 'Meanwhile the world goes on.' Mary Oliver. 'Wild Geese'. You know that poem?

Kate Maybe?

The sea crashes into the walls of the house. Then:

Chris They should have listened to you. The midwives.

Kate It's my fault. I don't communicate.

Chris You told them you were dying.

Kate They thought I was being dramatic.

Chris But you were dying. And so was your baby.

Kate Yes.

Chris And then they saved your life, and your baby, so you feel angry but also extremely grateful. It's confusing. And then your husband got home and he doesn't believe you.

Kate He also thinks I'm being dramatic.

Chris Very painful.

Beat.

And yet here you are. With a healthy child. And another chance at life. What a gift.

Beat.

Shall I make you a cup of tea before I go?

Kate I'd love a cup of tea but I can make it if it's too much trouble?

Chris Why would I offer if it's too much trouble?

Kate I don't know I'm just saying words . . .

Elaine enters, talking, wearing a dressing gown, headscarf and sunglasses:

Elaine I don't know about anyone else but I would benefit greatly from the dried-out testicle of a Sicilian bull.

Kate I'm sorry?

Chris How about a couple of paracetamol?

Elaine Ugh. I suppose it'll have to do. Chris doesn't believe in my traditional remedies, Kate, but then again nor has Chris spent a long hot summer shooting on the shores of Mount Etna drinking too much Campari. So what does she know?

Chris She knows nowhere within a thirty-mile radius sells bull testicles.

Elaine And there in a nutshell is what is wrong with the provinces.

Chris Cup of tea?

Elaine No thank you. How are you, my dear?

Chris She's spoken to Sue.

Elaine And?

Kate Good news!

Elaine Really?

Chris We've got interest from a big investor at a major studio. Sue wants us to put together a pitch for his team to read As Soon As.

Elaine I have no idea what any of that means.

Kate It means we have work to do.

Elaine We do? Did you hear that, Chris?

Chris I'll get you a paracetamol.

Elaine It's happening. It's really happening. Is it happening?

Kate It's a promising start. Do you still want it to happen?

Elaine I am a ballerina in a closed-up music box gathering dust. I am squashed down in the dark with a spring wound up beneath my feet and I've been staring at my own face in the cheap silver paper of a pretend mirror for thirty years. Are you really asking if I want someone to open the lid?

Chris Ballerina in a music box isn't free just cos someone opens the lid.

Elaine Course she is. She starts dancing.

Chris Only in circles.

Elaine She fulfils her essential purpose! Kate Trellis says we have work to do! Can you imagine how meaningful that is for a woman in my situation? People don't understand. They think it's a hobby. They sit in their offices twiddling pencils and taking meetings and they're happy to call it a job but the idea that what we do is work
    they find that laughable. But we know, don't we, Kate?

57

Kate Yes?

Elaine Yes yes YES!

Chris Here. They're past their sell-by date so you better take a few.

Elaine Are you leaving?

Chris In a minute.

Elaine You're not taking Kate Trellis.

Chris / Why would I be taking Kate Trellis?

Elaine She's to stay with me. Aren't you, Kate Trellis?

Kate If that's still okay?

Chris Rest before work please.

Elaine Nonsense.

Chris Kate?

Kate Got it.

Elaine Look at her. Such courage!

Chris Indeed.

Chris and Elaine gaze at Kate.

Elaine If only I had been born now. How different things might have been. Eh?

Chris It's not too late.

Elaine Perhaps not. Thanks to Kate. Thank you, my dear.

Kate What did I do?

Elaine You brought news from beyond the wall. You have inspired me. And given me hope!

Kate Aw.

Elaine There is work to be done! And life has new meaning!

And with this, Elaine departs. A beat. Kate laughs awkwardly. Chris smiles. Then:

Chris Your tea.

From the other room, Elaine begins practising the opening movement of Moonlight Sonata. Kate and Chris listen for a little while. Then:

See, in a way you're lucky cos
  it was something me and Connie always talked about
  starting again
  getting a place by the sea. But I was never ready. To leave
the city. And then she got sick so she never
  but also more to the point we never
  together
  we assumed we'd have the future. You do. Don't you?
Can't really live every day like it's your *last*. Be ridiculous.
You'd never change your knickers. Spend your life savings on
run-down cottages. But at the same time, it's like Elaine says
  what you need
  who you are
  you can't keep denying it. Maybe it's time to let go and
accept that you're a fool.

Kate Are you
  sorry are you calling me a fool?

Chris shrugs. Kate laughs. Then. Kate stops laughing.

Chris Your tea's here. I'm off.

Kate Okay.

Chris Tell Elaine I'll be back in a few days. And I'll get her
some wood. So she can stop smashing up the furniture.

Chris is leaving. When:

Kate Chris? Before you go. I'm
  I'm so sorry.

Chris What for?

59

Kate No I mean. About your wife.

A beat. Chris nods. Then. Chris leaves.
   Kate stands for a moment, listening to the music from the other room. She picks up her tea. She takes it over to an armchair. She sits down. After a moment, she hears a bird singing.
   She tries to work out where it's coming from. Then, turns suddenly to look at the cage:

Seriously, what the fuck?

She spills her hot tea on her trousers as Elaine's piano breaks into the frenetic third movement of Moonlight Sonata.

Argh!

Kate leaps up, pulls her trousers down around her ankles to escape the boiling material. She flaps and stumbles around.

Ow ow ow
   oh Christ

She bumps the table (or something) setting in motion a clownish sequence of events which ultimately result in the toppling of the standing lamp (or similar): the lamp falls into the fireplace and the bulb explodes in a shower of sparks. Then:
   Kate gasps. She stands up, trousers around her ankles, staring at the roaring fire now burning in the hearth.
   End of Act One

Act Two

7

Lyonesse.
 Different day. Afternoon. Chris is pottering in the kitchen bit. Elaine is standing by the fire.

Elaine We open on 'Elaine'
 (me)
 standing atop a cliff. Gazing out to sea. We understand her to be a complex woman. Strong. Stylish. Striking. But also: likeable.

Chris Uh-huh.

Elaine We pan back to the wider landscape. The sea. The sky. A large house, Elaine's home. And here begins this slow-moving, beautifully shot, expressionist piece in which Elaine, an ordinary, unknown woman goes about her quiet daily life: she lives alone, she works in a local shop, she swims every day. She is for the most part
 unremarkable. However
 as we watch, we start to get clues that all is not as it seems: the theatrical poster on the wall; a glimpse of an old TV show starring a woman who looks just like Elaine! We begin to ask: who is Elaine really? What is she doing here? What is she hiding? Then, a mysterious visitor arrives: a stranger: asking questions, and gradually we learn the truth: Elaine is on the run from her past, in fear for her life. Terrifying flashbacks start to intrude on the action, as Elaine remembers: she is being followed. We don't know who by, only that the stalker is relentless, unstoppable, his actions build towards the climax: the murder of the birds. Two meaty hands extinguish their precious lives, one by one, in real time. Feathers float through the air. Elaine, terrified for her life, flees and arrives by the sea.

61

Chris And?

Elaine And that's as far as we've got.

Chris Who's the mysterious visitor? Why are they here?

Elaine We haven't figured that out yet. As I said, we've been working extremely hard but there are as yet some details to be ironed out. Or 'finessed' as Kate calls it.

Chris And sorry what are we calling this thing?

Elaine It's called a 'treatment'.

Chris Huh.

Elaine Don't ask me why.

Chris Cos it's sort of like, 'How are they going to treat you?'

Elaine Not me, the story. Sue's very impatient to read it. She's been sending emails non-stop! She says this project has gone from a pea to a pumpkin.

Chris Is that good?

Elaine It appears to have lent some urgency to proceedings. Kate says we need to focus on 'pinning down' the um the um 'tent poles of the narrative turning points' and working out the action of the protagonist.

Chris Tent poles?

Elaine We need to clarify the sense of 'who Elaine is and what's driving her'.

Chris Well I'm driving you most of the time.

Elaine Ha. Well quite. Apparently 'Elaine' is too passive.

Chris Your Coke.

Elaine What do I want? Thank you. And what will I do to get what I want?

Chris Do you think Kate's okay out there?

Elaine I'm sure she's fine.

Chris Should I go check on her?

Elaine No! I need your help!

Chris What if she's drowning?

Elaine What if she is? You can't swim!

Chris I can call the coastguard.

Elaine It's okay, I can see her.

Chris Is she swimming?

Elaine She looks like she's waving . . .

Chris What?

Elaine I'm joking. The poem?

Chris I know the bloody poem. Let me see.

Elaine Look. There. She's a fine swimmer. Making her way back to shore.

Chris Okay. Good.

Elaine I don't know why she was so adamant she had to go swimming, do you?

Chris I do not.

Elaine Anyway, never mind her. Let's focus on what's driving me, so we can tell Sue.

Chris What kind of person is Sue?

Elaine How do you mean?

Chris Is she a kindred spirit?

Elaine I would think so.

Chris Does she have any pets?

Elaine We can ask Kate.

Chris Not that we can make judgements based on that. She might be allergic.

Elaine Kate says Sue is a vocal supporter of women. Everyone who works for her is a woman and she's really dedicated to telling women's stories.

Chris What is a woman though?

Elaine We are! Aren't we?

Chris I never really felt like a woman.

Elaine Didn't you?

Chris And some women

Elaine What?

Chris are not kindred spirits.

Elaine But Kate is. We know she is. Isn't she?

Chris Does Sue go to the hairdresser's?

Elaine Why does it matter?

Chris What colour are her office walls?

Elaine Focus on Elaine! What does Elaine / want?

Chris What do you want? You want to tell the truth about Clive.

Elaine Yes!

Chris And you want to triumph!

Elaine God yes! This can't be a tragedy. Elaine Dailey deserves to triumph! She must rise like a phoenix. Give hope to others who are still trapped by vengeful partners. It's not fair that we should have to wait for them to die before we can be free!

Chris It's the story of your release. From captivity.

Elaine But will they believe me?

Chris Don't worry about that.

Elaine It would kill me. You know that, don't you? To have waited all this time to feel safe enough to speak out, only to find I am not believed. I would swim out into the ocean and I would let the waves take me.

Chris You mustn't think that way.

Beat.

What happens next?

Elaine That's what I'm asking you!

Chris No I mean with this 'treatment'.

Elaine Oh. We're to deliver it tonight. Kate insists we must hit the 'deadline'!

Chris She's not what I expected.

Elaine Who, Kate? She's delightful.

Chris Been / a while since

Elaine And such good company. What did you say?

Chris Dunno. Just. Silly.

Beat.

Elaine I knew it! You've taken a shine to her.

Chris Sod off. / What cos she's a young woman so I must fancy her?

Elaine I knew this would happen! I said it the moment I met her!

Chris She's got a husband!

Elaine Connie had a husband. Till she met you.

Chris Not the same.

Elaine 'Oh Chris is so compelling!' I'm being Kate. 'She's so centred and reassuring and wise.' She's been asking about you non-stop. Wanted to know if you were any good. As a poet.

Chris What a strange question. What did you say?

Elaine I told her about your book. She wants a copy but I said she'd have to ask you since it's out of print.

Chris Maybe she wants to turn my poems into a movie.

Elaine I highly doubt it. She wants an insight into your very soul.

Chris Don't say any of this to her!

Elaine Why not?

Chris Because. She's here to make your film.

A long pause. They are both momentarily lost in their own thoughts. Then:

What if . . .
   At the end of the film, you go back to Elaine on the cliff. Full circle.

Elaine Yes.

Chris Are you / imagining it?

Elaine I'm imagining it

Chris The wind buffets her face and body
   brings tears to her eyes
   the sound of the sea's rushing in her ears
   and then suddenly
   it all shifts and moves and you realise she's not really on a cliff. She's on stage in the West End. And the sound you thought was the sea is in fact the roar of applause.

Elaine I like it.

Chris Yeh?

Elaine I like it. I'm just not sure it answers the key questions: what does Elaine want and who is the mysterious visitor?

At this exact moment, the door bangs open and Kate appears on the doorstep. Dripping wet and shrieking with cold. She has a towel and her mobile phone. As:

Kate OMIGOD I FEEL AMAZING.

Elaine To the fire!

Kate / I'M SO COLD.

Chris Come! Come!

Elaine Stand by the fire, Kate! / You must get warm!

Kate is so cold she can hardly speak, her teeth are chattering, her body shaking:

Kate That was
insane. I feel
incredible. My whole
body is
I've got like
omigod I'm cold
I don't think I've
ever been this

Elaine Here

Kate cold

Chris You did it!

Kate I did it!

Chris I'm so proud of you!

Kate I feel

Chris Do you feel amazing?

Kate Better than amazing!

Elaine You are overcoming, Kate Trellis. This is just the beginning!

Kate I thought I'd be swallowed up by the waves or or or washed away. I thought the cold would give me a heart attack or I'd get tangled in seaweed and drown or
   I stood there for so long
   trying to build up courage
   and then
   something inside me told me
   I had to do it. So I just
   I walked into the sea and I did it. I swam!

Chris A baptism.

Kate And then I phoned my husband!

   Beat.

Elaine What did you say?

Kate I broke up with him.

Elaine You what?

Kate I told him how unhappy I've been. And I told him it's over!

   Beat.

Elaine And what did he say?!

Kate He couldn't understand me
   at first because
   my teeth were chattering so hard
   but then when he understood, he got very angry. He said you can't just go away for a week and have a complete personality change, Kate. I said it's a spiritual transformation, Greg, and he said it sounds more like a breakdown.

Chris Huh.

Kate He said 'What about Izzy?'

Elaine What about Izzy?

Kate I said we could talk about all that further down the line. And he said 'Well good luck getting me out of my own home!' So I hung up.

Elaine Good for you!

Kate I can't stay married to him. He's a bully! I don't mean
   he's not a Clive Arbor or anything like that but there's
this selfishness in him and and and every time we argue he
adopts this position
   that I'm over-reacting or or or hysterical
   that he's reasonable and rational
   and I let him! I let him make me mad! Why do I do that?
Does he just want me to *feel* mad? Or does he actually *think*
I'm mad? I don't know. All I know is I'm so sick of trying to
explain myself to him! Is that mad?

Chris You're not mad.

Kate I feel less mad than I have for a long time.

Elaine I think you're extraordinarily brave.

Chris I agree.

Kate I think I'm going to pass out!

Chris Sit down. / Sit sit

Elaine Yes come and sit down.

They guide a chair towards her and guide her into it.

You have taken a huge step. This is an enormous decision

Elaine looks at Chris, slightly horrified.

Hopefully not a decision which will impact your ability to
work on my project?

Chris Elaine!

Elaine / What?

Kate Of course not! Your project is inspiring my decision! If anything I'll have more energy to dedicate to it. Although I mean obviously logistically there's a lot to sort out. Like who goes where and what if he really won't leave the house?

Elaine You can come and stay here!

Chris Yes!

Kate What about Izzy?

Elaine Bring her here! We can help.

Kate Bring Izzy here?

Elaine Why not? We love children, don't we Chris?

Chris We do.

Elaine I've got all these empty rooms.

Kate What about my job?

Elaine What about your job?

Chris Isn't this your job?

Kate Good point! This is my job! I can talk to Sue about working remotely or

Elaine To have a family! Here in the house! Can you imagine? I can read Izzy stories and teach her to dance! Chris can show her how to write poems and drive a car. And there's a playground in the village. And the beach. You can go to London as much as you need, Kate, and one of us will always be here to look after her! Doesn't that sound wonderful?

Kate I mean, yes?

Elaine She can have the little attic room looking over the sea. She'll be able to hear the wind-chimes as she falls asleep.

Beat.

Kate I guess maybe we could do that. If you're sure?

Elaine I'll go and get the room ready!

Kate Oh no, you don't need to

Elaine I want to! I think Little Izzy will find this house quite magical, don't you?

> *Elaine leaves. Chris and Kate alone.*
> *A pause.*

Kate I uh

Chris Batten down the hatches!

Kate Sorry?

Chris Storm on the way.

Kate Surely not. It's so clear out there!

> *Then: Kate's phone rings. She hurries to look at it.*

It's him. He can leave a message. Sorry Greg, but you've been an arsehole one too many times. I'm making a stand. At long last I am SETTING MYSELF FREE!

8

Lyonesse.
> *Early morning. Wind whips round the house. Rain pours. Elaine is placing buckets and saucepans around the room to catch leaks.*
> *Kate enters, energised. She is wearing one of Elaine's dresses.*

Kate You're up early.

Elaine The wind woke me. Look. Look at that sky.

Kate Gosh yes.

> *Kate looks out at the stormy sky.*

Where's Chris?

Elaine She's popped home to check on the cats. She's coming back.

Kate Chris has a cat?

Elaine She's got eleven.

Kate Eleven cats?

Elaine Why do you say it like that?

Kate It's just
  a lot of cats.

Elaine Not really. If you think about how many cats there are in the world.

Kate I guess.

  Pause.

I wanted to tell you together but

Elaine Tell us what?

Kate Sue read the treatment.

Elaine Already?

Kate She's an early riser. She read it on the treadmill at the gym
  classic Sue

Elaine And?

Kate and look I'm so sorry to do this but

Elaine Oh god

Kate she LOVES it.

Elaine What?

Kate She wants to buy it.

Elaine I thought you were going to say she hated it!

Kate I know! I did that on purpose!

Elaine Kate Trellis!

Kate I'm sorry. I'm just so excited. Listen to this: she's sent over a contract.

Elaine A contract?! What for?

Kate For your story. She wants to commit. To officially move this into development. You want to take a look? I've got it on my phone, we sign all this stuff digitally now.

Elaine I wasn't expecting a response so soon!

Kate Apparently the big boss at Pacific Studios has been literally hounding her about it. So Sue's like 'Get this baby locked in!' Here, take a look –

Elaine I need my glasses.

Kate You should send it to David. Get him to check it over et cetera. Here – read –

Pause.

Elaine No, I can't make sense of it.

Kate It's our standard contract for this kind of project, basically saying you agree that Lilith Entertainment own the rights to your life story, that you entrust us with the creative approval over any changes we need to make for the purposes of dramatisation all of which will be within reasonable limits and subject to good faith. In other words, you trust me, you know we're on the same page, I'll be your point person on the project, so if a writer comes on board and has any crazy ideas you hate or you feel are wrong, we'll be guided by you.

Elaine I see.

Kate You don't officially have what we call creative 'approval' but we'll do everything in our power to make sure you're happy. This is your chance to speak your truth, after all these years. So. Okay so here's the amount you get on signature, I know it's not much but obviously the real money comes further down the line and you can always get David to negotiate.

Elaine And what about my starring role?

Kate Oh we get to all that later.

Elaine So it's not in the contract?

Kate Not yet. This just gives Lilith the rights to tell the story. Casting is a totally different conversation so

Elaine Don't I want it in there now?

Kate I can certainly ask. To be honest, Sue might not go for it, but

Elaine Well no then. Don't ask. We don't want Sue to change her mind.

Kate I think we can cross that bridge when we come to it. And if we need to do a bit of work to persuade the investors then we'll do it. Right? We're not afraid of hard work.

Elaine Certainly not! We're afraid of many things, but hard work is not one of them!

Kate I just feel so good about this, Elaine. The timing. The fact that Pacific want to move fast. This project is our ticket to success and respect and and

Elaine How do I sign?

Kate Oh. I mean. Don't you want to speak to David?

Elaine I trust you.

Kate You don't want more time?

Elaine I want to sign it. I've got this feeling

Kate What feeling?

Elaine just a bad feeling. Like something's going to try and stop us.

Kate Who's going to stop us?

Elaine I don't know. I just think we should sign it now. Just in case.

Kate Yes? Okay amazing okay, let me find the
    I just need to
    uh let me just
    here we go. Here. You sign here. Are you sure about this? Because

Elaine signs the document with her finger.

Okay. Well.

Elaine And now you. You can't back out.

Kate I won't. I wouldn't want to!

Elaine You promise?

Kate signs the digital document.

Kate Here. Look. I'm signing here on behalf of Lilith Entertainment. And that's it!

Elaine That's it?

Kate We're making a movie!

Kate squeals with excitement.

Elaine I can't believe it!

Kate How do you feel?

Elaine I'm doing it, Kate. After all these years. My story will finally be told!

Kate And it will change the world!

Elaine And you'll be with me, right?

Kate Every step of the way!

Beat.

Are you okay?

Elaine I'm a passionate woman with a zest for life.

Kate You are.

Elaine But since I moved here, I've never been further than Tintagel. Never been back up to London. I've been gone from the world an awfully long time, you know. What if

Kate What?

Elaine What if I'm no longer spell-binding? What if I'm

Beat.

Kate You're going to be fabulous.

Elaine Am I?

Kate It's going to be everything you want it to be. And more. I promise. And you're not the only one who's scared. I'm terrified. What if I'm being horribly selfish? What if I'm ruining my child's life? Moving her here? Trying to make some kind of alternative

Elaine Why would moving here ruin her life?

Kate and then I think about this sense I've always had that that if only my mother hadn't had me, she'd have been happier. Or. Had a better life. And I don't ever want Izzy to feel that way. I don't want her to feel like I had to give stuff up for her sake. But the thought of trying to keep it all going on my own is

Elaine You won't be on your own.

Kate Kids need stability. And routine.

Elaine And love.

Kate What's the difference between security and and and conformity?

Elaine I'm not sure I understand the question.

Kate It's not a question, I'm just

Elaine Oh look. Headlights coming up the road. Chris is on her way back. What's she going to say when we tell her we've signed the contract?!

Kate We should celebrate.

Elaine Yes! You entertain Chris while I get ready. Make her a cup of tea but don't let her have more than four sugars. Then when I'm dressed we'll open a bottle of champagne!

Kate Good plan!

Elaine Oh, and: ask her about her poems! She wants to talk to you about them.

Kate Really?

Elaine Oh yes. She's very eager to get to know you better.

Elaine nods meaningfully. Kate laughs self-consciously. Elaine hurries out of the room.
    Kate dances over to the kettle. Fills it and puts it on the hob. She gets a mug out. Grimaces. Cleans it. As headlights illuminate the room. An engine still running.
    Kate checks her reflection. Fixes her hair. Then:
    A knock at the door.

It's open!

The door opens.

Greg Hello stranger.

Kate was expecting Chris, but it's Greg. He's wearing a trucker cap with some kind of American logo on it. The headlights from the car outside move away. The car is leaving.

See what you mean about that road. Jesus Christ.

Kate What are you doing here?

Greg My taxi driver was a lunatic.

Kate You got a taxi? From where?

Greg From home. I'd had a few drinks.
   What?!

He enters. Closes the door behind him.

Not going to give me a kiss?

Kate Why are you here?

Greg I've come to take you back.

Kate Where's Izzy?

Greg Oh *now* she's worried about Izzy!

Kate Where is she?!

Greg She's at home with your mother. Who says you need to get your fucking act together and come home. NOW. You've still got the hire car, I take it? I've sobered up now. I can drive.

Kate No.

Greg No you don't have the car or no I can't drive?

Kate No I'm not coming home.

Greg You don't have a choice. Get your stuff. Where are the keys?

Kate I said
   no.

Greg Kate?

Kate Don't talk to me like that. You're not my dad.

Greg No I'm the father of your child. The child you've *abandoned*.

Kate I've been gone for six days!

Greg What's going on here Kate? Can you please explain?

Kate There's nothing to explain.

Greg You said you were leaving me.

Kate I am leaving you.

Greg Why?

Kate Because. For lots of reasons.

Greg Where are you going to live?

Kate Here.

Greg You're planning to live here?

Kate Why not?

Greg Sue says you're obsessed with this house.

Kate You've spoken to Sue?

Greg I called her. After you dumped me. I said I thought you might be having some kind of a breakdown.

Kate You said that to my boss?
    You're lying.

Greg Apparently you've become very 'passionate' about this project. Sending her long emails in the middle of the night.

Kate Yes I am passionate about this project. Which is maybe why she's just sent the contracts over. And we've signed them! So

Greg Sweetheart?

Kate I'm an Executive Producer!

Greg You need help.

Kate Oh fuck off Greg.

Greg Pack your stuff and get in the car. I would like to drive you home where we can talk about this calmly. Izzy really misses you.

Kate Does she?

Greg She's been asking where you are.

Kate And what have you said?

Greg I told the truth. I said Mummy's having some problems.

Kate What would you say that for?

Greg I can't lie to her.

Greg takes his cap off. He holds his arms open.

I love you, Katie. You can't just phone me and tell me you're leaving. I'm your husband. We have hopes and dreams and plans. We have a life. Together –

Kate I don't want our life. Not anymore.

Greg Since when?

Kate And I don't want a husband.

Greg Well that's hurtful.

Kate I hate that word. It's a stupid
   annoying

Greg Stupid?

Kate I was so desperate to have a husband. Got to have a husband by the time you're thirty-one, Kate. Got to be pregnant by thirty-three. And now I've done that haven't I? And I've gone back to work because I can't just give up work. Got to do both! And now you've decided it's time to have another. Got to HAVE ANOTHER. Haven't we?

Greg I thought we wanted another?!

Kate You know what they keep saying to me?

Greg Who?

Kate People! Your mother. Your sister. 'Oh you'll forget the pain! It's nature's way. You forget the trauma!'

Greg I mean it is kind of a biological

Kate What's that?

Greg It's like a biological fact that women forget the trauma of childbirth.

Kate Is it? Well then I must be unnatural because I haven't forgotten! And you know what else I haven't forgotten?

Greg Oh my god. / This again!

Kate Yes! Yes! This again!

Greg I didn't know she was going to come early, Kate!

Kate You could have flown back sooner!

Greg It was a fifty-million-pound shoot!

Kate So what? / SO WHAT?

Greg So it's not that fucking easy! Okay?! The studio don't give a shit about my life. They don't give time off for sick babies or distressed wives. If I leave
I lose the job. Is that my fault? I don't think it is. But you're never going to forgive me for it are you? / You're never going to forget!

Kate Maybe I would forgive if you'd shown the slightest interest in hearing what I actually went through / without you

Greg Are you kidding? You've told me fifty million times!

Kate Fifty million pounds! Fifty million times!

Greg You know what I mean! And what do I say to you? When you tell me?

Kate You tell me it's a story with a happy ending.

Greg Because it is!

Kate You're only saying that because you want me to do it again!

Greg I'm saying it because it's a story with a happy ending!

Kate My vagina is broken! I can't

Greg Still feels pretty good to me.

Kate Oh go FUCK yourself Greg. You're a DICK.

Greg Can I say something?

Kate I nearly *died*. And you
weren't
there.

Beat.

I did everything right! I have done everything right
my whole life
and now I've had enough. I'm not doing it anymore.
I can't. And I don't have to.

Greg You don't have to. But you can't stay here.

Kate I belong here.

Beat.

Greg You belong in a creepy old falling-down house?

Kate It's not creepy, it's beautiful. I feel like myself here.
These people are my kindred spirits. They understand life in
a way you never will. They are artists.

Greg Who are?

Kate Elaine.

Greg You said these people?

Kate Elaine and her neighbour.

Greg And who's her neighbour?

Kate Chris.

Beat.

Greg Chris? Chris who?

Kate I don't know.

Greg Why has your face gone weird?

Kate My face / hasn't gone weird.

Greg Who the fuck is Chris?

Kate Elaine's neighbour.

Greg Is he now?
   And what? Are you sleeping with him?

Kate No!

Greg But you want to?

Kate I don't know. Maybe.

Greg Maybe? Maybe! Fucking hell. I don't believe this.
Have you actually lost your mind?

Kate I don't know! Maybe! Who would blame me?

Greg I can't / believe this is happening.

Kate If I left you on your own / as much as you leave me

Greg Are you seriously going to stand there, tell me you
'maybe' want to fuck some bloke then say it's my fault?
Because that's fucking gaslighting, Kate. That's psychopath
shit right there. Okay?

Kate You're the psychopath!

Greg For what? Because of what?

Kate Because all you see is yourself! You don't care about me!

Greg Then what am I doing here? Huh? Why am I here? If
I don't care?

Kate I don't know! Because you don't like losing control.
Because you don't like the idea that I can just leave. Who's
going to pick up the slack, Greg? Who's going to hold the fort?

Greg I'm here to bring you home. And I'm not leaving
without you.

Greg sits down in an armchair.

Kate Can you get up please?

Greg No.

Kate Get up!

Greg I said no! I don't care what bullshit you make up to try and get rid of me. I don't care what insults you throw at me. I'm your husband. / And I'm not

At this moment, Elaine, now dressed and ready, enters.

Elaine Oh! I thought / I heard voices –

Greg bounces back up again.

Kate Elaine!

Elaine We've got company! Who's this?

Kate and Greg's demeanour instantly shifts into a more socially acceptable couple vibe.

Kate This / is Greg.

Greg Hi. I'm Greg. / Kate's husband.

Kate Greg this is Elaine.

Elaine Greg Trellis? The famous film director?

Greg Kate's husband, yes.

Elaine Delighted to meet you, Greg. I wasn't expecting you. / Is this

Kate I wasn't expecting him either. He came to uh surprise me! He missed me! Didn't you sweetheart?

Greg I did. Terribly. I've come to take her home.

Beat.

She has to get back to London.

Kate It's just that

Greg We have a child. So

Kate That's right I should uh
Izzy's been asking for me so

Elaine I see.

Beat.

Is everything alright, Kate?

Kate Oh yes! Everything's great.

Elaine Can I offer you a drink, Greg?

Greg Yes why not?

Kate Darling?

Greg What darling?

Kate If you're driving back to London

Greg I can have one drink, darling. I would love a whisky
please, Elaine. If you've got it?

Elaine Certainly.

Kate Bit early for a whisky, Greg!

Elaine Oh we don't worry about such things at Lyonesse.
Time is an illusion
as are all things. Right, Greg?

Greg I wouldn't go that far.

Elaine You've come from London, Greg? This morning?

Greg I have, yes.

Elaine You must have set off in the middle of the night.

Greg Well I was eager to see my wife, Elaine.

Elaine How romantic.

Kate He got a taxi the whole way.

85

Elaine Good gracious! That must have cost a fortune! Sit! Sit!

Greg Thank you. It did. Not to mention the roads around here are terrible.

Elaine Oh I don't drive. I have to wait for a lift with / my neighbour if I want to go by car.

Kate I don't think the roads are that bad.

Greg Your neighbour?

Kate A bit narrow maybe?

Greg How lovely to have such a kind neighbour.

Elaine Oh yes Chris is a kindred spirit!

Greg is staring at Kate. Kate looks away. A moment. Elaine presses on:

I was in love with a film director, Greg. Once upon a time.

Greg Ah yes! Clive Arbor, right? I'm a huge admirer of your husband's work. He was a true legend. A great loss to the British film industry.

Elaine mixes Greg a drink. It takes a while. As:

Elaine Not technically my husband. But we were together for three years. I was still married at the time. I know, shocking isn't it? I had a husband
and I betrayed him for another. Poor Hal never got over it. And to be honest with you, Greg, nor did I. Hal was a wonderful man and a terrific actor. He was a lot older than me though, and I'm afraid I did get rather bored. Went off in search of adventure and let's just say it didn't end well.

Greg Does it ever?

Elaine Excellent question. Does it ever?
I think it does. The difficulty for us women, Greg, is that stories so quickly spiral into morality tales, don't they? You tell a story about a man having an adventure

if things go wrong that's just part of the journey
your drink

Greg Thank you.

Elaine but for a woman, as soon as anything goes wrong
for her
   we start to read into it all sorts of warnings. We're so
obsessed aren't we with how women should behave. And of
course we internalise that narrative, don't we Kate? We
blame ourselves.

Greg Cheers.

Elaine It's very hard for you to understand that, Greg
Trellis.

Greg I think I understand it pretty well. Men blame
themselves too. Increasingly I think we're being told we're to
blame for most things. Aren't we?

Elaine Are you?

Greg I don't think we are. I just think people would like to
think we are.

Elaine People?

Greg The evil white man. To blame for everything now, isn't
he?

Kate Greg?

Greg Cancel culture. Me Too.

Kate You're in favour of those movements, obviously.

Greg Oh obviously.

Kate They're a good thing.

Greg They had good *intentions*. But now we're at the point
when someone can just sling an accusation at a bloke
   he doesn't even need to be alive anymore

Kate Greg?

Greg and everyone jumps on the bandwagon, starts calling him an abuser or a rapist or whatever with no evidence whatsoever

Elaine Do they?

Greg So my only argument against all this brilliant stuff which don't get me wrong is brilliant and I'm totally in favour of it
 but my only argument against it is
 you must have evidence. It can't just be her word against his. Otherwise it's not fair is it? It's just slander or

Kate It's much more complicated than that, I think.

Elaine Do you?

Kate Much more.

Elaine Because what if there isn't evidence?

Kate Doesn't matter.

Greg If there isn't evidence, you should keep quiet. That's my opinion.

Kate We don't need to listen to his opinion.

Greg Come on Kate, you must agree a society in which a man can be tried and convicted and sentenced to oblivion without a scrap of evidence is a slippery fucking slope!

Elaine Another drink, Greg?

Greg / Thank you Elaine, very kind.

Kate I think the point is we need to widen out the argument and start taking into account the fact that these kinds of accusations don't always have an evidence-based whatsit or

Greg Whatsit?

Kate I mean there isn't always going to be evidence, is there?

Greg Course there is. If something *happened*.

Kate What if what happened is complicated?

Greg If it's complicated then maybe it's not black and white and if it's not black and white then maybe

Greg yawns widely.

no one deserves to get cancelled?

Kate What if the evidence has been destroyed? Wait, hear me out
for example this girl I knew at university, she had her drink spiked by some guy she met in a nightclub and when she woke up there was like (sperm) in her trousers and she kept those trousers for literally *years* thinking maybe one day the guy would be caught? But then she watched that Marie Kondo programme and decided to throw them out because they didn't bring her joy.

Greg I mean that's just utterly
I can't even
why would you destroy evidence of your own rape?

Greg yawns again.

Kate Because it's not logical, Greg. Okay?

Greg Women aren't logical? You can't say that!

Kate I'm saying being a victim makes you act in a way which might not seem logical to an observer. And the patriarchal, adversarial legal system which insists on

Greg does a loud snore.

setting opposing sides up against each other in an attempt to oh haha very funny, yes I'm so boring aren't I? I didn't start this conversation by the way you did so the least you can do is have the decency to
Greg?

He is asleep.

Elaine I think he might be asleep.

Kate He's pretending. Isn't he?

Elaine I don't think so.

Kate Greg? Are you okay?

Elaine It is an awfully long drive.

Kate I know but

Elaine And he has been looking after that child of yours, hasn't he?
   He must be exhausted.

Elaine and Kate look at each other.

Kate I'm so sorry about this. I had no idea he was coming.

Elaine Is he very angry?

Kate Not with you.

Elaine Should we call the police? Let them know there's an angry husband on the loose!

Kate I mean

They look at Greg, snoring in the armchair.

Elaine He'll wake up. Then what?

Kate I'm going to have to go with him, aren't I?

Elaine No!

Kate He won't leave without me!

Elaine I'm going to suggest something
   because I don't know your situation
   all I know is the situation I've been in for the past thirty years and how I wouldn't wish that on anyone Kate so if you want me
   to help you
   throw him over the cliffs

Kate No! / What?

Elaine If that's what you want.

Kate You didn't put something in his drink did you?

Elaine Like what? Absolutely not!

Kate No okay, sorry.

Elaine I just don't want you to feel alone. If you need
you know
rescue.

*Kate stares at Greg. For a fleeting second, she imagines it.
The freedom of it. The relief. And then, almost as quickly,
the unimaginable horror –*

Kate I don't.

Elaine I don't want him to hurt you.

Kate He won't.

Elaine Don't go back with him.

Kate I don't know what else to do.

Elaine You don't love him.

Kate It's complicated.

Elaine You don't need him.

Kate Don't I?

Elaine Stay here. With us.

Kate I wish I could.

Elaine What's stopping you?

Kate stares at Greg. The freedom. The relief . . .

Kate I don't know. I feel confused.

Elaine Because of Chris?

Kate What? No. What about Chris?

Elaine I suppose it just seemed to me like

Suddenly the door opens, and Chris is back.

Chris I had a bath and fed the cats then I thought I'd better get back before the road floods.

Elaine Chris! Thank goodness you're back!

Chris What's all this?

Elaine This is Greg Trellis.

Kate My husband.

Elaine He's trying to take her away.

Kate He says he won't go without me. And he's left Izzy at home with my mum.

Elaine I vote we chuck him off the cliff.

Chris Elaine!

Elaine Kate says no.

Chris Of course Kate says no. We can't do that.

Elaine Why not?

Chris Because we're not cold-blooded murderers!

Elaine I don't want him to take her away.

Kate I don't want to go.

Chris He'll go without you, won't he? If you say it and really mean it.

Kate I don't think he will. And I can't just leave my mum with Izzy.

Elaine Your mum's with Izzy?! But that's perfect! Call her! Get her to bring Izzy here.

Kate She won't. She's already cross with me for staying down!

Chris Can't you fetch Izzy and bring her here?

Elaine Yes! Do that!

Kate What about Greg?

Elaine Chris can take him to the train station. Put him on a train.

Kate Oh god.

Elaine If you go now, we'll make sure he can't catch up with you.

Kate What will I say to my mum?

Elaine The truth! She's your mother. She's hardly going to take his side, is she?!

Kate Actually she almost always takes his side!

Elaine Then you need to tell her what he's really like. No?

Kate is struggling to think.

Anyway. You can think about it on the way. The important thing is to fetch Izzy. Go!

Kate No okay it's just, I wanted to prepare her. Give her time to

Elaine She'll think it's an adventure!

Kate What about all her toys? Her friends at nursery? I can't just

Chris We're rushing her, Elaine. She's getting scared. Don't be scared, Kate.

Greg makes a noise, a scared little whimper.

Elaine He's dreaming.

Chris Bad dream, it looks like.

Kate Poor Greg. He looks different here. Smaller.

Elaine It's not okay just to turn up like this. It's frightening.

Kate I'm so sorry. It's my fault.

Elaine It's not your fault. It's his fault.

Kate I don't know what to do. I felt so sure before but

Suddenly Greg sits up, terrified, as if waking from a horrible dream:

Greg OH GOD!

Kate Greg?

Elaine Uh-oh.

Greg What happened?

Kate You fell asleep. / You were dreaming.

Greg I was dreaming. I was dreaming. Jesus that was so real I thought

Kate Are you okay?

Greg My head hurts.

Kate Do you want some water?

Chris I'll get him some water.

Greg Who's that?

Kate That's Chris.

Greg That's Chris?

Greg laughs.

That's *Chris*?!

Kate Don't.

Chris comes back with a glass of water. Offers it to Greg.

Chris I'm Chris. Here –

Greg looks at Chris.

Greg Hi Chris. No thanks.

Kate Take the water.

Greg I don't want it.

Kate Thank you Chris.

Kate takes the water.

Greg Great to meet you, Chris. I've heard a lot about you.

Chris Likewise.

Greg Oh yeah?

Kate Greg?

Greg Yes Kate?

Kate gives Greg the water. He takes it.

Kate That's enough. Drink your water.

Greg drinks his water. They all watch him.

Better?

Greg Guys, would you mind if I just had a little chat with my wife?

Kate No, that's okay

Greg Could we have some privacy?

Kate This is Elaine's house! / We can't just

Chris Sure. We'll let you talk. Come on, Elaine.

Elaine Really?

Chris We'll go upstairs. You take your time. All I'm going to say is this:
     in this weather
     that road floods fast, so if you do want to get back to London today

Greg Thanks Chris, that's so kind of you.

Kate Greg!

Greg What?

Chris Elaine?

Chris reaches out a hand to Elaine. She takes it. They leave up the stairwell.
After they are gone, Greg turns to Kate.

Greg Did that crazy old bitch spike my drink?

Kate No! / What are you on about?

Greg Because if she did I am fucking calling the police, Kate. You can't just do that to people and get away with it!

Kate Course she didn't!

Greg Then why did I fall asleep like that?

Kate Maybe because you've been up all night?

Greg I had a dream you were chucking me off the cliff.

Kate Did you?

Greg It was so real. Christ I can still
you dragged me to the edge of the rocks and I couldn't stop you
I had no control over my body
kept trying to kick you off but I had no feeling in my legs
and the look on your face it was like
and suddenly I was over the edge and just plummeting towards the rocks and the crashing waves and then I woke up like

Beat.

Are you gay now?

Kate No!

Greg But you fancy that Chris person?

Kate No! I don't know!

Greg Oh my god. You do?!

Kate I don't fancy her exactly or maybe I do I just feel inexplicably

Greg What the hell is going on? This is madness!

Kate Hush!

Greg Can I talk to Kate please? My Kate. The real Kate. Kate who spends four hundred pounds a month getting her highlights done. Kate who took six pairs of heels on our glamping holiday.

Kate No I didn't!

Greg Kate who reads the Bodum catalogue for fun!

Kate It was three pairs.

Greg Kate who made me rip out our entire kitchen because she said it was disgusting!

Kate That kitchen was disgusting, Greg!

Greg This fucking kitchen is disgusting, Kate! Look at it! Look at the floor! This place is filthy. There's water coming through the ceiling! And look at the state of you, what are you wearing?

Kate It's one of Elaine's. It makes me feel magical.

Greg Well you look insane.

Beat.

Sorry but you do.

Beat.

You've got the perfect life, Kate. How can you not realise, most women would kill to be you?! You're gorgeous. Successful. You've got a great husband. A fantastic kid. A top job. A three-million-pound town house in a fucking affluent part of London. A cleaner! A nanny! No one in their right mind would chuck all that away to go and live in a dirty fucking hovel with a couple of crazy old bats! How are you going to work from here? What are you going to say to Sue? And what about Izzy? You can't bring our daughter into a place like this. You'll have social services on your case. I'll call them myself if you even think about it! Kate. Look at me. Look at me! I want my wife back. And Izzy wants her mummy back.

Beat.

What's this really about? What's going on? You can tell me, Katy.
You have to tell me or I can't help you.

Beat.

Kate (I don't want to have a baby.)

Greg What?
What did you say?

Kate You heard!

Greg No I didn't! I literally didn't hear what you said / can you just

Kate Why though? Why can't you just hear me the first time? Why do you have to make it so hard for me?

Greg I don't

Kate I don't want another baby!

Greg But

Kate Okay? I don't want another baby, Greg! I wish I did but I don't! I can't! I can't go through it again! And I know it means Izzy won't have a brother or sister and I do feel sad for her but at the same time I want her to have a mother who can function. So
so there you go.

Beat.

Greg I see.

Kate Do you?

Greg Maybe we don't have to decide now?

Kate I want to decide now. I will only come back

Greg Yes?

Kate If you promise we don't have to have any more children. I want to delete the app. I want to go back on the pill. I want to take this promotion and not have to stress out about maternity leave. I want to enjoy Izzy. I want her to be enough. If you want more children, you'll have to find another wife.

Greg Another wife can't give Izzy a brother or sister.

Kate Well
turns out
nor can I.

Pause.

Greg Fine.

Kate Fine what?

Greg If this is what it takes to get you home, then fine. I do think it's not a good idea to make decisions when you're having a breakdown but

Kate I'm not having a breakdown. I'm saying NO!

Greg Okay.

Kate You hear my no?

Greg I hear it.

Kate And you won't make me say it again?

Greg What do you mean?

Kate I find it very hard to say no, Greg. It costs me every time. It makes me feel guilty and exhausted and

Greg I think you need to work on that.

Kate Yes probably.

Greg Because that's not my fault, Kate. You can't blame me for that.

Kate I'm asking for your help. Please don't make me keep saying no.

Greg Alright. I said I heard you and I heard you. You won't have to keep saying no.

Kate Thank you.

Kate nods. She goes over to her bag. Takes out a set of car keys.

Can you wait in the car?

Greg Are we leaving?

Kate I need a few minutes to pack my stuff and say goodbye.

Greg But you're coming with me?

Kate Yes.

Greg Because I really do love you.

Kate I know.

Beat.

I love you too.

Greg What are you going to say to Chris?

Kate Nothing.

Greg Don't be doing any kissing!

Kate Shut up!

He heads out of the door. He has forgotten his cap.
The door slams.
Kate stands for a moment. Then:
Elaine and Chris come rushing back in.

Elaine She's still here!

Chris We thought you'd gone!

Elaine You got rid of him?

Kate He's waiting in the car.

Elaine What for?

Kate I'm going with him.

Elaine Oh no!

Kate It's the right thing to do. For Izzy. And he's agreed we don't have to have another baby. So.

Elaine What about the rest of it?

Chris Elaine

Elaine She said he was a bully!

Chris She's made her choice.

Elaine What about the work? Our work!

Kate I'm not giving up.

Elaine He'll make you.

Kate He's not like that!

Elaine Isn't he?

Chris Elaine! She's made her choice. We're not going to try and change her mind. It wasn't easy for her, was it Kate?

Kate shakes her head.

You must do what you think is right. And we support you.

Kate I should grab my stuff.

Kate leaves up the stairwell. Elaine and Chris look at each other.

Elaine Is there nothing we can do? What if he hurts her on the way home? Stops the car

strangles her by the roadside
dumps her body

Chris We have to trust that Kate Trellis will overcome.

Somewhere outside, a flock of geese passes. Honking loudly.

Elaine But will she?

Chris Look. Geese.

Elaine Oh yes.

Chris and Elaine watch the geese for a moment.

Chris See?

Elaine Yes, yes. Geese. And?

Chris And, I'm talking about the significance of the geese.

Beat.

Elaine Dailey wants to tell the world about Clive Arbor. She wants to rise like a phoenix from the ashes. She deserves to triumph. This is her time to step into the light. Your time to be the protagonist. Your time.

Elaine The protagonist would pick up that axe
pull that jumped-up little toadstool of a man out of his car
and whack his head off in a single blow. Wouldn't she?

Chris I suppose that's one option.

Elaine What's the other?

Kate comes back in. She has changed out of Elaine's dress and is back in her own clothes. She's carrying her leather weekender. Maybe she's brushed her hair.

Kate I put your dress on the end of the bed.

Elaine You can keep it.

Kate It's okay. Thank you though. Oh look, Greg's left his cap. I better

Kate picks up Greg's cap. She struggles to fit it into her bag. It's painful. She drops things. They watch her. When it is finally over, she turns to Chris and Elaine. A beat. Then:

You don't need to look like that. I'm coming back! We'll be working together all the time. This is just the beginning!

Elaine The beginning. Yes.

Kate I won't let you down.

Elaine Come here –

Elaine goes over to Kate. They hug.

I love you, Kate Trellis.

Kate I love you too. You've changed my life.

Elaine And you mine.

Chris You should go, or you won't get down the road.

Kate Chris?

Chris Yes?

Kate It has been a pleasure to meet you.

Chris You too.

Kate I'll see you again?

Kate reaches out a hand. Chris takes her hand. They shake hands.
There is the faint sound of wind-chimes. Magical. From somewhere out in the rain. Then:

I'm sorry I couldn't

Chris You were

Kate I feel like

Chris I think

Kate I could have

Chris No no

Kate I just

Chris Kate?

Kate I'm not like you.

Chris In what way?

Kate I don't know.

Kate lets go of Chris's hand.

I should go.

She picks up her bag and goes to the door. She opens it. A gust of wind and rain blow in.

I'll uh – I'll see you soon.

*Kate hesitates on the doorstep.
Then she leaves. The door closes.
Chris and Elaine go to the window. They watch the road. Then:*

Chris Ah! Forgot to give her this.

Chris takes a small book, published in the eighties, out of her pocket.

Elaine Is that your book of poems?

Chris You said she was interested.

Elaine You've still got time to catch her?

Chris Nah. It's okay. I can give it to her next time.

Elaine Do you really think she's coming back?

Chris I do. I believe it. I believe in Kate Trellis.

9

Lilith Entertainment.

Sue is waiting. After a few moments, Kate bursts in through the door, wearing a loose-fitting summer raincoat, wet hair, shaking an umbrella.

Kate Ugh! Can you believe this weather?! Could someone please alert British Summer Time that it's meant to be August? I'm so sorry I'm late. Greg had to get an early flight and the nanny's not well and Izzy had a meltdown about me going! I've had about five minutes of sleep –

Sue It's fine.

Kate I'm insanely hormonal

Sue Kate?

Kate and it takes me about half an hour to walk to the tube so

Sue Shall we make a start?

Kate Right! Sorry I'm just
all over the place

Sue Please stop apologising.

Kate Sorry.
Sorry.
Let's make a start.

Beat.

Your skin looks amazing by the way.

Sue Thank you.

Kate I love that suit.

Sue So.

Kate Right.

Sue Elaine Dailey.

Kate Yes. Yes!

Sue We told Buddy we'd have a script by the end of May. What's taking so long?

Kate I'm trying to get all my ducks in a row!

Sue I've got David Pritchett on the phone every day wanting an update! It's been months, Kate. We need to pick a writer!

Kate It's hard to find the right person!

Kate takes her coat off. Underneath, it is now possible to see that she is very pregnant.

Sue What happened with Mike French?

Kate Well. Okay. So. Mike went down to meet Elaine.

Sue Sit down. Okay. Good. Did you go with?

Kate I couldn't because Greg was away, but

Sue How did it go?

Kate I spoke with Elaine afterwards and she loved him.

Sue Great!

Kate And then I spoke to him

Sue He'd be *fabulous*.

Kate yes but he has some reservations. He isn't keen on the birds. And I said to him I do think the birds are quite a big thing for Elaine.

Sue Why isn't he keen?

Kate He thinks we've seen birds before.

Sue But he loves the Hitchcock angle, right?

Kate Yes he mentioned you and him had talked about that and he likes the Hitchcock angle but I said we don't want to

go down the route of making Elaine crazy and he said 'she is a bit crazy though'. And I feel like
my gut's just telling me he's not quite right. I think we need a writer who just

Sue But Elaine likes Mike?

Kate she does, but

Sue I think we should give him a shot. See what he comes up with. Buddy loves his stuff.

Kate it's just

Sue He's such a talent.

Kate it is a woman's story.

Sue Is Mike suggesting otherwise?

Kate Not at all, it just seems like he wants to change it.

Sue He's not changing it he's developing it.

Kate I just think maybe we should be looking for a woman?

Sue You've been out to women, haven't you? I thought they all said no.

Kate There's a few more on that list I sent you?

Sue Buddy didn't go for them. In fact he told me (in block caps) to 'QUIT FARTING AROUND'.

Kate But

Sue It's not like we haven't tried, Kate. And nine months down the line, we are in danger of losing Buddy. You know what he's like! And besides, look, I don't think we need to be gendered about it. This is a woman's story because it's about a woman. I don't think only women can tell women's stories do you? What about *Anna Karenina*? What about

Kate No of course, I just

Sue Mike French is a wonderful emerging talent. And you told me Elaine is more than happy to work with a man because for her it's about finding a what does she call it?

Kate 'Kindred spirit'.

Sue There we go!

Kate Yes but

Sue You know what I think? I don't think this is about Elaine. I think this is about you. You don't want to let go.

Beat.

I hope she's not making you feel guilty about going on maternity?

Kate No! No it's nothing like that. She doesn't uh
    I haven't actually told her yet so

Sue She doesn't know?

Kate I wanted to tell her in person. But then Greg was so busy I couldn't get away and suddenly it was five months and then six and

Sue Oh Kate.

Kate I just don't want her to think I'm abandoning her. She's so invested!

Sue Aren't we all?!

Kate It's just as soon as we hire a writer she's going to want to talk about casting and

Sue So we'll have a conversation with her about casting! She's not stupid. She'll understand. We all want this project to move forwards. Don't we?

Kate We do.

Sue So. In the spirit of progress, I've got something to run past you. How about . . . if we ask Greg to come on board. Wouldn't that make you feel better about letting go?

Kate My Greg?

Sue Buddy's keen.

Kate You mean to direct?

Sue Of course to direct! He called me the other day about this Polanski remake he's been shopping around, I said it's not for us Greg but we do have this Arbor project on the go. Pinged him over the treatment and he had some fantastic thoughts. He said old Elaine Dailey is far less interesting than her younger self, so why not foreground the flashbacks and make it predominantly a period thriller? Which I think is brilliant. He wants to use the house as a framing device but bring Clive's storyline right up in the mix, to counteract some of Elaine's passivity? Ramp up the tension. And he's got some very useful ideas about how to sidestep some of the legal issues, since all our lawyers have managed to dig up are a few disgruntled actresses, none of whom are prepared to go on the record.

Kate Have they?

Sue Which is no bad thing from our POV cos as Buddy said: 'Me Too's been done to death.' And listen I know what you're going to say, 'Shouldn't we get a female director?' but the thing is, Kate, Mike French buzz-buzz and safe pair of hands Greg Trellis. That combo could get us over the line with Pacific. And surely Greg's a 'kindred spirit'. Isn't he?

Kate I I I I I just need time to process.

Sue As you know, Greg's got a slot in Jan. Mike's itching to get started. And confidentially, Buddy's lining up some top-secret A-lister to play Clive. Get a fabby cast on board and suddenly we're all systems go. Shoot early next year. In the UK, maybe? Greg said you'd be cock-a-hoop about that. And great news for Elaine, no?

Kate Right. But

Sue Or do we want her to flounder in development for the next five to ten years?

Kate No of course not.

Sue How old is she now?

Beat.

We have to be practical. Yes? Realistic. This isn't about what Elaine thinks is best. It's about what's best for Elaine.

Kate Is it? Or is it about what's best for Lilith?

Beat.

Sue Well. I'm pretty sure only one of them will still be here for you at the end of your maternity leave. Or do you think Elaine wants to put her entire life on the back burner until you're ready to come back to work?

Kate No of course not / but

Sue But you do want to come back to work?

Kate I do I just

Sue Good. Listen. This was a tricky project with an unpredictable asset. You earned her trust. You got us a great deal. And we're going in with Pacific Studios. You've done a fantastic job, Kate. Elaine Dailey should be extremely grateful. She's lucky to have had you on her team. Okay?

Beat.

Why don't you let me speak to her? I'll give her a call in a couple of weeks when we've got a firmer update. When's your last day?

Kate Friday. But it's okay. I should speak to her. I'll give her a call this afternoon.

Sue Just do it now. Get it done. Why wait?

Kate You're right. I'll give her a call and I'll be really clear about
everything we've said and why and

Sue You'll feel better as soon as you've spoken to her.
I promise. And look. There's going to other movies. Okay?
Other life stories, if that's what gets your juices going. We'll
find you something you can be just as passionate about.
Soon as you get back. And in the meantime
take as long as you need to focus on that little baby. Boy
isn't it?

Kate Uh-huh.

Sue You got a name?

Kate We can't agree.

Sue Maybe when you see his face.

Kate Oh Greg will get his way. In the end. He always does.

Sue Izzy excited to have a little brother?

Kate Not really.

Sue laughs.

Sue Oh god when I had Chloe, Charlotte was furious. She
tried to kill her you know? Several times! It was hilarious.

Kate She tried to kill her?

Sue She couldn't stand her.

Kate But they get on now, right?

Sue Now? Now they're just in their bedrooms the whole
time on their respective devices. I don't think they speak to
anyone never mind each other!

Sue laughs.

Anyway, sweets, I've got another meeting, so I'll leave you to
make your call.

Kate Okay.

Sue You've done so well, hun. It's not easy, is it?

Kate No?

Sue Proud of you!

Kate Are you?

But Sue is already gone.

I just – actually – Sue? Can we just –? Can we . . .?

But Sue does not return. Kate stands for a moment. She takes out her phone. She places it on the table. She stares at it. Perhaps she hears the sound of the sea. Through which the thudding rush of a baby's heartbeat over an ultrasound. She touches her belly.

10

Lyonesse.
  Wind blowing. Dark skies. Elaine stands by the window. Chris hovers.

Chris What did she actually say? In terms of

Elaine It's all about budget, apparently. And algorithms.

Chris Algorithms?

Elaine This is according to Sue.

Chris What kind of algorithms?

Elaine To find out which actor is going to bring what value to a project in terms of numbers
  and who is 'meaningful' and in what location? And that's sort of how a lot of the casting works these days, so because I have no value
  if I want it to get made, I can't be the star.

Chris And what does Kate think about that?

Elaine Well this is what's confusing. Sue said the reason why she's calling and not Kate is because Kate has gone on maternity leave.

Chris Kate has? Why would Kate go on maternity leave? That doesn't make sense.

Elaine According to Sue, Kate left work on Friday and she won't be back for an extremely long time. If ever.

Chris But Kate's not pregnant. She can't be!

Elaine Obviously she can be, because obviously she is!

Chris Did you trying phoning her?

Elaine Several times. It says 'the person you are calling is not available'.

Chris She would have said though. Wouldn't she?

Elaine I thought it was strange she hadn't been back down to see us.

Chris I just assumed she was busy. Or that Greg didn't want her to come.

Elaine Oh I haven't even told you the best part yet. Guess who Sue wants to have as our director?

Chris Who?

Beat.

No.

Elaine It's a conspiracy.

Chris Kate would never agree to that! Surely!

Elaine And guess what. Greg Trellis and Mike French
 that writer we met who seemed so lovely? Greg Trellis and Mike French have done a new treatment. And Greg Trellis and Mike French don't like the birds.

Chris Don't like them how?

Elaine They want to change it. To a baby.

Chris What do you mean?

Elaine Their idea is that Clive killed an actual baby.

Chris Whose baby? Yours?

Elaine They think a baby is more powerful.

Chris Is that legal though? To say Clive killed a baby.

Elaine Doesn't matter. Because we're never going to know if he did or didn't. I come home and find the baby dead. And I blame Clive. But apparently what's so brilliant about this idea is we might
we might think
it was me. That I killed my own baby. Or we might think that none of it ever really happened
and that I made the whole thing up.

Beat.

Chris Is that what she said?

Elaine She kept going on about Hitchcock. A growing sense of madness. Apparently Greg *loves* the gothic creepiness of the house which is like 'a character in its own right'. I said 'the house isn't a character'. She said 'but it's a metaphor isn't it' and I said 'it's not a metaphor, Sue, it's my home. And the characters are me, Elaine Dailey, and my ex-lover Clive Arbor who killed my BIRDS and threatened to murder ME. That is the story.' She said 'it's not personal, Elaine. It's just that life and drama aren't always the same thing.' I said 'alright then, what if I change my mind?' And she said 'about what?' And I said 'about telling my story'. And she said 'well of course that's up to you. I'll check the contract, you can probably get it back in turnaround in a couple of years, but it depends when we signed off on the treatment.' And then she said I mustn't get the wobbles just because there's been a change of staff. We're still fully invested in the project, Kate just has to focus on her baby now so

Chris Invested?

Elaine I said 'Invested?' I said 'this is my TRUTH, Sue. It burns from inside my soul.' She said 'yes, Elaine. We all understand how important this is to you. We are one hundred per cent committed to helping you realise your vision. That's what we do here at Lilith Entertainment. We tell women's stories. Ask anyone, she said. That's who we are. We're on your side!'

Beat.

Chris Maybe Kate's been fired. They could be lying to us. She wouldn't just go on maternity and not even call. She knows what this means to you.

Elaine Perhaps Kate isn't the person we thought.

Pause.

Chris I'm trying to think of a poem –

Elaine NOT NOW!

Pause.

Will you feed the birds? I want to go for my swim.

Chris I don't think you should.

Elaine doesn't move.
A pause. Then:

Elaine I told you they wouldn't believe me.

Pause.

I'm going. I need to submerge my brain.

Chris You should wait. You're upset. And it's choppy out there.

Elaine Is it? Good.

Chris I don't want you to go.

Elaine I know, but I must.

Chris Elaine?

Elaine Yes Chris?

Chris You're my best friend. My only friend.

Beat.

I believe you. I have always believed you.

Beat.

Can't that be enough?

Elaine I wish it could.

Chris I should stop you.

Elaine You can't. You must let me go.

Chris You will fight though.

Elaine Maybe I'm tired of fighting.

Chris We all are. But we keep fighting.

Beat.

I know you, Elaine.
 You will.
 You will fight.
 You will fight!

Elaine takes a deep breath. Chris watches her. After a moment, Elaine moves to the door.

I'll light the fire. I'll feed the birds and put the kettle on. Make you a nice hot cup of tea. For when you get back.

Elaine goes. Chris stands for a moment. Scared what Elaine is going to do. Should she go after her?
  She goes over to the window. She stares out. Then she squares her shoulders. She must pull herself together. She puts the kettle on. She starts trying to light the fire. At some point, fiddling with the kindling, she starts to weep. Her hands are shaking. She gives up.

The kettle starts to whistle. Chris goes over and turns it off.

She remembers the birds. She goes and fetches the bag of birdseed. Scatters seeds into the bottom of the cage.

Here we are, lovelies. Are you hungry? Are you?

Will you sing for me? Sing me a song. Would you?

The birds do not sing.

Here you go, look. I'm going to open the door, okay? I'm leaving it open.

You can go now.

Go on. You're free to go!

The birds do not fly.

The waves crash against the side of the house. The wind whistles.

Chris sits down in the armchair to wait.

The End.